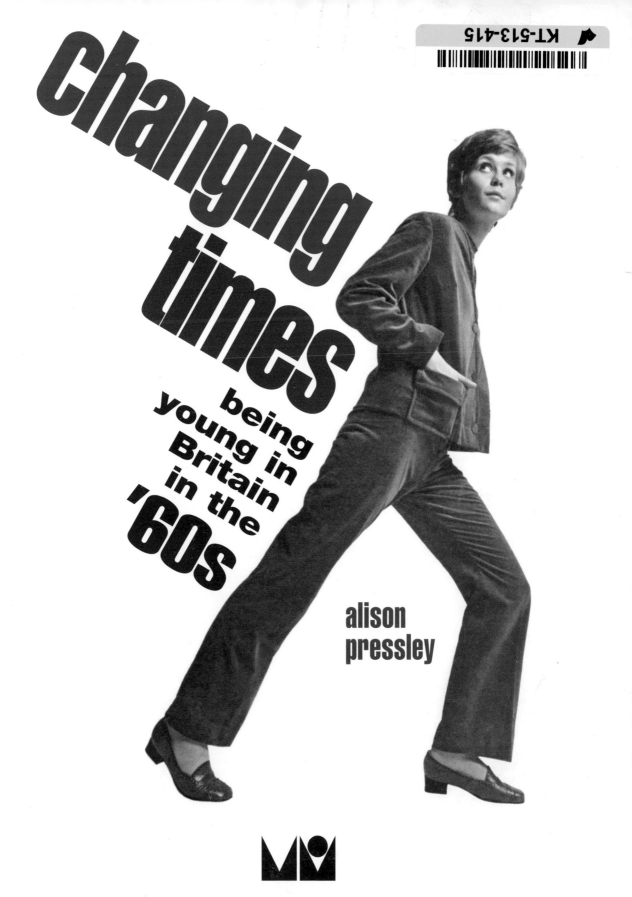

changing times

being young in Britain in the '60s

alison
pressley

Picture Acknowledgements
The publisher would like to thank the following for supplying photographs and illustrations for this book:
Advertising Archives : 68 top,104 top, 112
Corbis Bettman: 6, 11, 14, 19, 28 right, 30, 31, 38, 63, 76, 77, 78, 80, 84, 99, 101
Hulton Getty: 41, 42, 43, 67, 82
PA News Agency: 21, 31 right, 34 top, 46, 47 below, 110, 111
Popperphoto: 58-59, background, 60 top
Syndication International: 97 *Daily Express*
Courtesy of Richard Adams Associates: *Oz* cover, 52

Special thanks to Audrey Slaughter for the loan of her personal archive copies of *Honey* and *Petticoat* magazines.

The publisher would like to thank Ron Callow, Nigel Fountain, Richard Margrave and Judith Palmer as well as the author and the author's friends for the loan of personal photographs and memorabilia, and apologizes if the name of any individual contributor has been inadvertently omitted.

First published in Great Britain in 2000 by
Michael O'Mara Books Limited
9 Lion Yard
Tremadoc Road
London SW4 7NQ

A CIP catalogue record for this book is available from the British Library

ISBN 1-85479-578-3

1 3 5 7 9 10 8 6 4 2

Designed and typeset by Design 23
Edited by Gabrielle Mander

Printed and bound in Singapore by Tien Wah Press

dedication

To Alan and all the others who made the sixties great

acknowledgements

As for the previous book in this series, *The Best of Times*, I would like to acknowledge my debt to Helen Townsend's book *Baby Boomers*, published by Simon and Schuster in Australia in 1988, which provided the inspiration and the role model for this book.

Nearly all of the people who featured in *The Best of Times* also submitted cheerfully to my video camera for *Changing Times*. I also called on the memories of many additional friends. Here are the names of those whose memories make up the bulk of the text. My heartfelt thanks to them all.

Derek Barton, Christie Brown, Wendy Canning, Jenny Cattell, Mavis Cheek, Tom Dack, Carol Dix, Joyce Foley, Peter Garland, Neal Gordon, Trevor Grove, Cliff Hall, Simon Hopkinson, Mary Ingham, Roy Jackson, Pat Kirby, Ray Kirby, Elaine Lister, Caroline Lurie, Heather McCauley, Frances McKenna, Janet Prescott, Jennifer Roberts, Rosalind Snaith.

My thanks also to my friend Carol Dix for permission to quote from her book *Say I'm Sorry to Mother* (Pan Macmillan, 1979). Stories from people who were famous or beginning to be famous in the sixties, luminaries of the time, are scattered through the text as 'Days I'll remember' boxes. Huge thanks to my sister Valerie Grove for leaning on her friends and acquaintances to provide these stories, and of course thank you to those famous people. Finally, thanks to Gabrielle Mander and Lesley O'Mara of Michael O'Mara Books for their faith, support and professionalism.

introduction

People told me *ad nauseam* that there was no point compiling a book about the sixties, because the sixties had been done to death. They were wrong. The sixties from the point of view of fashion models, rock stars, magazine writers, movers and shakers and other high-profilers living in Swinging London *have* been done to death. But what about the impact of the sixties on the lives of ordinary young people – kids from the provincial towns and suburbs like thee and me?

The sixties were the heyday of youth power. Those of us who were children in the fifties reached our teens and twenties in the sixties – and we found ourselves in the middle of a heady explosion of colour and sound and creativity the like of which our flabbergasted and frequently outraged parents had never seen.

Like most decades celebrated for their mood, their certain style, the sixties didn't really start until well into the decade, about 1963. Before then, the mood was very much that of the fifties. Rock music was still essentially pop; fashions were leftover Teddy boy and girl stuff; public

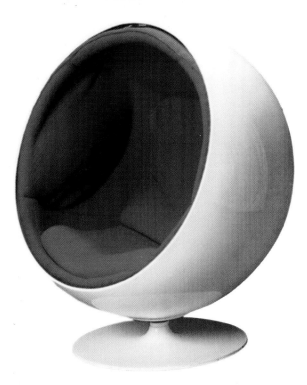

puff of marijuana, or steadfastly refusing to do so... getting wheels, breaking loose, taking off...

As in my previous book, *The Best of Times*: *Growing Up in Britain in the 1950s*, the idea in *changing times: being young in Britain in the 1960s* is to paint a portrait of a decade in a series of vignettes and anecdotes. Nothing heavy, nothing academic or anthropological. Just our stories. I hope you relive your own glory days as you read the funny, sad, touching and occasionally cringe-making reminiscences of twenty or so ordinary people who were young in Britain in the sixties. Our memories were shared by millions, and they accompany us as we gently f-f-f-fade away.

ALISON PRESSLEY, FEBRUARY 2000

morality was firmly entrenched in the traditional strict not-until-you're-married attitude. Then roughly when the Beatles first became popular, everything changed. The youthquake hit, and nothing was the same again, ever. In the sixties the times were, in all respects, a'changin'.

What was it like to be young in the sixties in Hull, Newcastle, Worcester, Farnham? Going to the first boutique to open in Birmingham... the frisson felt by London girls when the buzz about Biba got around... screaming at concerts in Wigan... doing the twist at dance-halls in Bolton... being persecuted by the headmaster because you dared to be the first boy at your school to get a Beatle haircut... taking that first

Step out in Donbros Springthings and make the ColourMates scene

contents

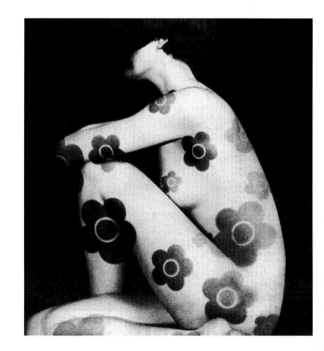

Everything had felt so Victorian in the fifties. It really was as though everything burst into colour when the sixties and the Beatles and their music came along.

1960 was a changeover year in my life, from the dagginess of being a child in the fifties in that monochrome world to a world full of excitement. The satire boom happened around then. It was a period of becoming genuinely politically aware. You started the sixties drinking Vimto and by the end you were drinking crème de menthe.

Generally, there was a feeling of 'we can have a good time for as long as we want'. It was an endless party. Getting a job and other such issues were on the sideline.

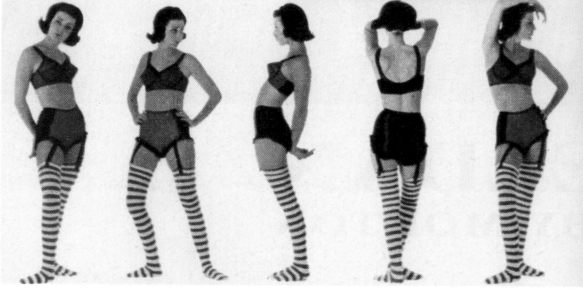

23rd APRIL 1966
ONE SHILLING

for the young and fancy free

petticoat

Beauty stays clinging ... Sweater Dresses
go swinging ... and Undies get a new break

You were absolutely allowed to have fun and experiment. Generally speaking, everyone was having a good time. There were lots of parties, with masses to drink and decorations all over the place. There was no sense it was going to end; none at all.

Experimentation. The feeling that you could live on the edge, that it was wide open, that you were actually living in a very interesting time. Maybe you were just lucky that all these things were happening. There was lots of style, lots of things were happening, and it was all worth involving yourself in.

As a period in history, it did seem like a huge liberation. It seemed to belong to the young, and I was one of them. Even then, I was aware of being in the right place at the right time, and there was a certain pleasure in knowing that.

It was the feeling that you could wake up in the morning and think of an amazing idea, and you could do it. Nothing was daunting, everything was possible. People

weren't hindered by their accents any more, whether they were northern or Cockney or Antipodean or whatever – in fact an accent was an advantage, for the first time ever. There was a recognition that it was what you did, not who you were or what your voice said about you, that was important.

Regional awareness came in with the Liverpool thing, the Newcastle thing. Suddenly, it wasn't a source of shame that you came from somewhere north of Watford. Suddenly, there was the world, and you could go and join it.

PHILIP NORMAN

Philip Norman, biographer of the Beatles, Buddy Holly and Elton John, was a provincial journalist in Darlington until 1966 when he won, with a profile of his grandma, a feature-writing job on The Sunday Times Magazine. *In his Beatles biography he says: 'For those who grew up in the 1960s, 1967 is a year to be remembered above any other, the moment when their own youth reached a dazzling and careless apogee, the year of love, peace and flower-power.'*

"As a rule, only war, or some fearful tragedy, can penetrate the preoccupations of millions in the same moment to produce a single, concerted emotion. And yet, in June 1967, such an emotion arose, not from death or trepidation, but from the playing of a gramophone record. There are, to this day, thousands of Britons and Americans who can describe exactly where they were and what they were doing at the moment they first listened to Sergeant Pepper's Lonely Hearts Club Band. That music, as powerfully as Kennedy's assassination or the first moon landing, summons up an exact time and place, an emotion undimmed by time or ageing."

...DAYS I'LL REMEMBER...

It was a bit of a blur. It just rolled on.

We grew up assuming we could have our freedom and adventures, and come out unscathed, didn't we?

What we didn't know was that it was The Sixties. We just thought, 'well, here it is and here I am'. There'd been the Depression, then the War, then the age of austerity, and now, we felt, 'it's going to be good for ever and ever'. We didn't think, 'oh, I expect it'll go back to being dreary'. We thought, 'goody, we've solved things'.

I was very aware that it was a significant
era. I thought we were the bee's knees. I
thought we were the first people ever to be
like that, we'd broken all conventions, we
were going to change the world, we were
untouchable. I thought everyone who came
before us had missed out. We were dead
lucky. Nothing would ever be the same
again, and my generation had done it. I was
living in the best times there had ever been,
and my generation was the best that had
ever lived. We thought differently, we were
different – no question.

I can't think of a better time to have been young. Everything was still so naughty: you didn't easily grow your hair, you didn't easily smoke pot, you didn't easily leave home; you didn't easily tell your parents that you were going to live with a girl or that you were gay. So many things that you did, like going to a pop concert or hitchhiking or wearing funny clothes, were considered on the edge; you were being deliberately rebellious.

It was a good time, wasn't it?

It was fab!

The look

Our appearance—the clothes we wore, how we arranged our hair, what we slapped or grew on our faces—was what the sixties were all about. This was what distinguished us from 'them', the pitiable people who didn't belong to our generation. As soon as we were let loose from smocked party dresses and navy serge short trousers we gleefully invented our own special look. It started in the late fifties with the full skirts and drainpipe trousers of rock 'n' roll, gathered momentum in the mid sixties when psychedelia meant we went out looking like optical illusions, and came to fruition in the late sixties in a cloud of floating chiffon, beads, jangling bells, bell-bottoms, sequins and embroidered kaftans. We left a trail of flowers in our wake.

From the fifties...

The fifties was an era of poverty, and a hangover from the war; dullness, essentially, despite the beginning of rock 'n' roll. Fashions seemed prissy, hairstyles were horrible. With the sixties, in came long straight hair, black polo-necked sweaters, skinny ribs – a more interesting time.

I couldn't wait to get into a roll-on. I'd watch the older girls at school enviously as they changed for PE. Then the minute I was old enough, tights came in and roll-ons rolled away forever, and I never did get to squeeze myself into a corset. I could do with one now, though.

When tights first came onto the market, I never knew whether you should wear them under or over your knickers. It was never very plain, was it? And there were two schools of thought about it. I was seriously worried at the time.

When I was fourteen, in 1961, my school organized a Christmas dance. My aunt was staying with us at the time, from the deep north, and she and my mother said they'd go shopping for a dress for me. I got home from school on the day of the dance, all agog, and found that they'd bought me a frilly little girl's dress. I knew how much it hurt them, but I just couldn't face going to the dance in that revolting dress. So I ended up going in my usual weekend wear, a checked skirt and striped top, feeling ordinary but at least not mortified. They were genuinely trying to do the right thing – they just had no idea that times had changed.

I spent most of the weekends of my mid-teens slobbing around my long-suffering parents' house in a smelly, stained, pale blue, quilted, nylon housecoat. They were all the rage at the time.

In 1961 my boyfriend bought me a white plastic handbag for my birthday. It was hideous, made me feel about fifty years old, but I had to cart it around just to please him. Then, thank god, leather shoulder bags came in and we could all ditch those awful handbags.

In the early sixties you bought your shoes – white sling-backs, with kitten heels – from Lilley & Skinner or Freeman, Hardy & Willis, and they cost 39/11, 49/11 or 59/11. There was a huge difference, depending on what you paid: 59/11 was really for best.

Do you remember those circular wicker baskets girls used to carry? They were like wicker hammocks. They went with the beehive, the sugared petticoat, the stiletto heels where the leather had worn off and the silver showed through, and lots of eye make-up.

SPRING INTO COLOUR WITH
little X by Silhouette

I can remember when striped socks were supposed to be in. I got red and white striped socks, and I went to a school dance thinking I'm bound to crack it here, I've got these amazing socks. But of course no one could see them. I went around tapping people on the shoulder and lifting my trouser leg and saying, have you seen my socks?

We'd spend all week working out what we'd wear at the dance hall. These were the days before jeans came in. For one dance, I wore a navy blue Marks & Spencer pleated terylene skirt, a thin pink wool round-necked jumper and a navy blue Orlon cardigan. I thought I was It. My friend was more arty-looking, because she was doing art: it rubs off. She was wearing a John Lennon cap.

Until about 1963, the casual gear we were expected to wear at boarding school consisted of a cravat and a Harris tweed jacket, then it suddenly changed to a roll-necked sweater, donkey jacket and desert boots.

Beatniks

I had an older brother at university when I was thirteen in 1960, and he would bring all these wonderful, exotic women home with him at the weekends. They wore black clothes and were going to become lawyers and doctors and so on. They were incredible role models to have; I was always ahead of my contemporaries because of them.

I desperately wanted to become a rebel, a beatnik, so I wouldn't have this grammar-school, middle-class girl image any more. I wore a lot of make-up, grew my hair long, wore jeans with bells on the ends and floppy sweaters – the whole beatnik trip, superficially. It's amazing to look back and realize how innocent it really was. Only a coffee bar, no purple hearts even. And how fantastically evil I thought it was.

I was always in complete awe of the beatniks. They were that much older than us, and seemed so much more sophisticated and intellectual, being into jazz and Sartre and Kerouac. I never dared to join them or be like them. But when the hippie movement came along I felt, yes, this is mine, and embraced it as much as I could.

I remember the coffee bars of Soho and around that area, central London. The first venue I ever went to was one of those folk places, full of people with beards and unkempt clothes, wearing berets, carrying folders of their artwork, having poetry readings.

We began going to folk clubs to hear the ideas of the beatniks. Dylan happened at that time and I got carried away just to hear the sound of his voice: the rasp, the wail, and the comments about war and peace; going to New York, Greenwich Village, coffee bars. That was the world I wanted.

The coffee bar in Stratford-on-Avon where I went to live in 1963, was called the Pit and was in at the beginning of the 'beat' circuit: St Ives, Brighton, Folkestone or Stratford, were the places where the beat with his bedroll and his newfound philosophy temporarily landed. The Acropolis in Folkestone was where you saw all these people wearing bleached jeans.

Beatnik men put on Dylan's 'man of constant sorrow' style, pretended to a depth of despair they couldn't really know, and it was a great turn-on. I used to think, when I was seventeen, that only men could really feel deep, philosophical sorrow. I used to fancy the moody type—all that angst and pain.

I went through a beatnik stage, via the San Francisco poets. I even had a record of Jack Kerouac reading his poetry with a piano background. *On the Road* was the bible.

My first boyfriend had been a chorister in the church I attended. Then the next time I saw him I nearly fell off my bench outside the pub, because he'd grown his hair, and he had a beard, and he smoked reefers and drank red wine straight from the bottle. He took me to a party; I went to C&A and bought a black cocktail frock with a lacy collar, so I looked like a deb and he looked really Bohemian, and we marched off to this party clutching two litre bottles of red wine, both of which he drank.

Mods and rockers

Be as free as a bird, Leggy girl

Just slip into Berkshire pantie stockings and show the world a lovely leggy suspender-free leg ... then walk free. Prices from 12/11 - 18/11.

in pantie stockings

BERKSHIRE **B**

Mods were essentially from London and the South-East; everywhere else was a different world. We were followers of fashion. We used to go to the Ricki Tik clubs in Guildford and Windsor to see bands like Georgie Fame and the Blue Flames, R&B-type bands. We never ate anything, because we lived on purple hearts, a mixture of amphetamine and barbiturates. You had to have a Lambretta GT 200, with a flat side, or a Vespa GS 160 with a more bulbous back. You had to have lots of fur all over it: fox tails, and fur down the sides.

If you were on a GT 200 you had to have a pillion passenger, leaning right back with their arms folded. Their function in life was to gesticulate wildly when you went past a rocker café like the Ace on the North Circular Road or the Manor café at Blackwater. Then the rockers would all jump on their bikes and chase you. One friend used to have this spray can, I don't know what it was, hair spray or whatever, but it was very inflammable. The pillion passenger used to squirt it into the exhaust of the scooter and get this huge flame-thrower coming out the back.

KINK THINK: THIS 'TERYLENE' IS SMOOTH

'Smooth,' said Dave of the Kink when he saw Ina in her 'Terylene suit. 'Still smooth,' they both sa a dozen pictures later–after lots of sitting, kneeling, curling-up actio But then 'Terylene' has never crushed, never needed ironing after washin

TWIGGY LAWSON

Twiggy was launched at age 15 in the Daily Express *by Deirdre McSharry with Barry Lategan's photograph – with mod haircut and thick black eyelashes – and the headline 'This is the face of 1966.'*

"I was a mod – you were either a mod or a rocker – and the mods' bible was *Ready, Steady, Go*. You just didn't miss it. I can remember the excitement on Friday afternoons, coming home from school, because this was *Ready, Steady, Go* night – 'the weekend starts here' – yeah! Mods changed their clothes style almost every week, which was difficult, as I was a young (13–15-year-old) schoolgirl and Mum and Dad couldn't afford to keep buying me things. But luckily I could sew and would copy the clothes I'd seen on the older girls. Some of the 'must have' items I remember were brown Hush Puppy shoes (can you imagine, on the end of my skinny legs!), grey calf-length pleated skirt and a navy-blue nylon mac – an absolute must, even in winter. We'd freeze to death, but we were *in*."

...DAYS I'LL REMEMBER...

Rockers were essentially working class, because they came out of Teds in the fifties. They hated fashion; they were stuck in a time warp from the fifties. Their hairstyle was always the same, a greasy ducktail with Brylcreme. They were into drink and leathers, they liked Elvis and they went to places like the Agincourt ballroom in Camberley. They liked greasy food, cafés with juke boxes. And every rocker wanted to own something like a Triumph or a Norton 650. They were always aggressive. Once I was in a rocker café and one of them said to me, 'You eyein' up my bird?' I said, no; he said, 'You sayin' she's ugly?'

As a rocker you could have whole conversations just in letters and figures, such as:

    'That a DBD 34?'

'DB 32.'

'With the double-R T2 box?'

'Yep.'

'Does that have the GP carb, then?'

'Nope – 10TT9. Your bike that T120?'

    'Sort of – it started out a T110, but I gave it a Bonnie 9-stud head, twin Monoblocs, 10 to 1 pistons, ES3142 cams...'

    And so on. If the bike was respected, so were you, generally, and I never saw much in the way of trouble. The loyal girls from the pillions – also in black leather and jeans and boots, usually with long blonde hair – sat around faithfully, saying very little indeed (you should have heard them on 'Terry' and 'Leader of the Pack', though) until it was time to follow their bloke out, wait for him to fire up the bike, and climb on the back again. Then off.

...into the sixties

I had skirts that stuck out with net underneath; a hangover from the fifties. But that changed with the Beatles, and also when Britain became a bit more European. We started to wear darker clothes. I remember being very proud of an outfit that consisted of a grey skinny-rib, a grey flannel skirt, really nice brown suede clumpy shoes –

because suddenly clumpy shoes came in, things you could walk in instead of horrible pointy things that you couldn't walk in. All my clothes became moody, beatnik style: black, grey, brown, how French girls dressed.

You could wear minis, or long skirts. There was suddenly much more flexibility. You could wear Courrèges or Mary Quant-style geometrics, sharp and neat and plain, or hippie-style things. There was a huge variety. I got my Courrèges-style boots from Russell & Bromley. Peter Robinson, Top Shop and Miss Selfridge started up.

Black polo-necked jumpers were totally in when the Beatles came in. You had to have one.

I remember feeling very marked out being the only girl in town with a Beatle jacket. It was in black suede and I bought it with my first Saturday morning job earnings, along with my first pair of black, knee-length 'kinky' boots.

My two best friends and I all had PVC macs, red, yellow and blue. And we each got a fur-trimmed bonnet.

Levi's were 32/6 or 37/6, one pound seventeen and six, and you could buy a belt for five shillings. You had to sit in the bath until they shrank, and copious amounts of dye came out – the bath was left dark blue.

I was going down to London to meet a pop singer for a date so I sewed along the seams of my jeans when they were on, to make drainpipes. I couldn't get in or out of them: they were completely skin tight. I didn't go to the toilet all evening – I couldn't. But when we went to a hotel to spend the night I had to unpick the seams to get undressed. I hadn't

taken a needle and thread to sew them up again, so the next morning they were a mess. He had to buy me a dress so we could go to his concert.

I wore so much eye make-up. Tons of dark brown eye shadow, eyeliner drawn all around, false eyelashes on top and painted eyelashes below, like Julie Driscoll. I sashayed into the student union one day and a (male) friend said, 'Hello, walk into a door did you?'

I used to buy fashion magazines more for wishful thinking than anything, and people like David Bailey changed the look completely. Clever, arty photography came in, making fashion more accessible. Twiggy and the Shrimp looked like normal people instead of haughty, upper-class clothes horses. They were ordinary girls from the suburbs; they were young, they were like us. It meant we could all aspire to interesting things. The world opened up. It was a very exciting time.

My friend went to London and came back to Wales wearing white boots with cut-outs, like the Courrèges ones, and masses of eye make-up, including false eyelashes and painted-on eyelashes underneath, and white lipstick. I thought she looked fantastic. I went to London, too, and bought myself a white PVC mac with black buttons from Miss Selfridge. Everyone asked me where my crossing sign was because I looked like a lollipop lady.

I remember big clip-on plastic earrings, Paco Rabanne style. I bought loads of them, mostly from Woolworths. Those and chain belts, and handbags with chain straps.

We all wanted to look like the girls the Beatles went out with – Patti Boyd, Jane Asher.

Hair

Everybody went out with their hair backcombed and frizzed and lacquered, and I remember the first person we saw who had a Mary Quant hairdo. It was dead straight, with a fringe, and came under her chin in a bob. We were amazed, especially when her hair moved when she danced. We'd spend all day getting ready to go out on Saturday night – there were girls who went shopping on Saturday mornings with rollers in their hair. We never stooped to that. When we'd finished backcombing we'd spray with this cheap lacquer that meant your hair was totally stiff and solid. So when we saw all the lads looking at this girl whose hair moved when she danced, we thought, maybe we should be doing something like that instead of all this ridiculous backcombing.

there was any moisture in the air whatsoever (which there always was) the whole lot would be drooping down, straight as a dye, by the time you got to the corner of your street – or, worse, *one* side was. Why we thought flick-ups were the thing I'll never know, because it's a very unnatural thing for hair to do, isn't it? It was such a relief when Sandy Shaw and Cathy McGowan came along and made straight hair okay.

The Beatle haircut was actually long-haired and bold then. They did create a whole new style.

'Flick-ups' were a disastrous hairstyle for those of us with dead straight hair. You had to spend all night in agony with those plastic rollers with spikes making sleep almost impossible, and in the morning you'd find that one piece of hair flicked up more – or less – than the others. Then if

When my hair got below my ears, I was thrashed and dragged over to the barber's for a pudding basin by my father. I didn't speak to him again for two years. Whenever he walked into a room, I walked out.

My friend Marion went to Vidal Sassoon's in London one weekend and had her hair cut into this brilliant geometric shape.

I had my hair cut by Vidal Sassoon himself, and I remember coming out of the salon and thinking, God, I look just like everybody else. You were just churned out.

I used to get into heaps of trouble about my hair. Teachers took it upon themselves to be hair monitors – or rather, hair dictators. You know: 'You can't play for the first eleven at football if you don't get your bloody hair cut.' But as long as I didn't look square, I didn't really mind. You had to have your hair a *little* bit long, otherwise you were branded as square, or weird.

Viva Biba!

We lived in a flat in Kensington Church Street, near a beautiful grocer's shop, which eventually became the new Biba. I used to use the grocer's, which had marble slabs and wonderful old characters in starched white aprons. We lived a few doors up, in a cul-de-sac called Holland Place Chambers. Ezra Pound had a flat on the top floor, and the Moody Blues started from there. So you'd see this old van parked on the pavement in this tiny cul-de-sac, with *the Moody Blues* written all over it in wonderful psychedelic lettering. Then one day the grocer's shop closed down and it was converted into an amazing clothes shop.

When boutiques like Biba opened you felt as though the whole world had opened up, too. You had to have long, straight hair, and big sooty eyes, and pale lipstick. That was Biba.

I used to go to Biba when it was in Abingdon Road, Kensington. It was like a temple. Because I was a single mother I didn't have a lot of money, so I'd buy things like beads.

My sister took me to Biba just after it opened. It was such an exotic place. Barbara Hulanicki would sit and sew up the hem for you herself, once you'd bought a dress. My sister bought a beautiful black dress with lace on the bottoms of the sleeves. My first Biba dress was an orange patterned mini. I felt so sophisticated and stylish when I wore it in Manchester – it was from the trendiest London boutique, after all.

BARBARA HULANICKI

Barbara Hulanicki was the founder of and genius behind Biba.

"One of my marvellous moments was the first time one of our mail order things just took off. It was 1963 and I designed a little gingham shift dress with keyhole at the back and matching kerchief. The offer was splashed across half a page of the *Daily Mirror*. We had a mail order address in Oxford Street, and normally we got about two or three hundred orders. We drove to Oxford Street and my husband Fitz went to get the mail – and he came round the corner and he was dragging three SACKS of mail, his face a beaming moon. We had 17,000 orders for that dress, all in 25-shilling postal orders. Fitz took them to Barclays Bank and they said, 'Sorry, we're not accepting this.' So he went round to the Nat West and we stayed with them for ever more.

That little gingham dress was like winning the lottery – it meant we'd got it right. I'd been doing fashion illustration before that, and I had to draw the dreadful clothes available then: terrible shapes, badly cut, unwearable. The next year, 1964, we opened our first Biba shop in Kensington, and two years later the bigger Biba in Church Street. We had a whole load of jersey dresses arrive that hadn't been properly stretched first and we were horrified to see the skirts were crotch-high. But the girls flocked in and leapt on them – we couldn't believe it – and we never looked back."

...DAYS I'LL REMEMBER...

I remember my mother saying, when I left school, that I should always buy good quality, timeless clothes like classic tweed skirts, Pringle sweaters and so on. But times had changed, and this kind of advice was completely irrelevant. I mean, I was wearing Biba paper dresses. You bought them for three quid and wore them two or three times – maybe even once, depending on what you spilt on them – then tossed them out. I had a lovely pink one; I was sorry it was paper, actually, because I could have kept it for ever. You had to wear a petticoat underneath, and they were pretty uncomfortable, and you couldn't wash them, of course, but they looked great.

I had a lilac Dr Zhivago coat from Biba, with black frogging. I thought I was the bee's knees. It hid everything too, which was very useful.

In the mid-sixties, the whole of West London was seething with beautiful people. Everyone had heard of Biba by then, and we thought, why don't we open one in Birmingham? So we did. We'd go into Biba every week and see what fashions were in. We had to adapt them all for the Birmingham market, because they hadn't even seen their knees at that stage, let alone their crotches. We had to introduce tights, because they were worried about people seeing their underwear. It was called The Alley, and all the Birmingham girls would bring their mothers and boyfriends with them every Saturday. We had music, and magazines, and places for people to sit. It was a complete breakthrough in terms of shopping; it was a happening, Birmingham's first boutique. We held an outdoor fashion parade in the Bullring in

1966, with music and posters and razzamatazz, and it was such a new thing to do.

One garment I remember, when Barbara Hulanicki went into longer stuff, you had a hook-y thing that came over your finger, like a ring. Long sleeves, with this V at the end hooked onto your middle finger. That was so elegant.

There were tops and dresses that you didn't have to wear a bra under. That was quite a breakthrough: we'd only just come out of the era of whirlpool bras.

For the first time, people didn't want expensive clothes that would last a long time. They wanted something fashionable that would last

a couple of weeks, then they'd move on and buy something else. Colour, instant fashion, being trendy.

Mini skirts

We were wearing mini skirts in Britain long before anyone else was. Jean Shrimpton may have caused a big sensation in Australia when she wore her mini to the Melbourne Cup in 1965, but I'd already caused a minor sensation in Paris that year. We were so used to them that we forgot how extraordinary people elsewhere found it, seeing young girls wearing strips of material that scarcely covered their bums.

Mini-dresses in hot summer weather were quite something. Boys used to say the girls were coming out in their flowery knickers on the first day of warm weather. I enjoyed the 'flasher' feeling, I loved wearing those short, revealing dresses.

I was at a party in New York early in 1966 and at one stage I was surrounded by men, who were trying to measure how far up from my knees my skirt came. I think it was about four and a half inches. Some of the older guys were just about apoplectic. Luckily I was there with my parents, otherwise I probably wouldn't be here to tell the tale.

My sister gave me a fantastic Indian mirror-patterned jacket in 1966. I wore it as a mini dress, and it only just covered my bum. It had sleeves, so you couldn't raise your arms when you wore it, because if you did, you'd be arrested.

Mini skirts were great fun. But we kept hearing about girls who wore mini skirts in the winter getting an extra layer of fat on their thighs, to compensate for the cold. This was a bit alarming, and may have prompted maxi-coats, do you remember them? So you wore your micro mini skirt, with tights, and over it a huge maxi coat to keep warm. And, of course, boots.

Cool

In 1966, in Carnaby Street, I bought a blue short-sleeved shirt with epaulettes and a button-down collar, pale blue denim slacks, denim-y canvas shoes and a blue peaked cap. I got clip-on sunglasses for over my glasses. Then I bought *Steppenwolf*. So you bought all this stuff and you just knew you were now *it*. Everything's going to change, everything's going to be fine. I went to Hampstead Heath, it was a sunny day, and I remember sitting there waiting for it all to happen, waiting to be transported off into this world of models and fashion photographers and pop stars.

You conned yourself that by wearing your black PVC raincoat and your sunglasses, you were part of the revolution.

I remember walking through Kensington Market and seeing a pair of beautiful mustard yellow ankle boots, with platform soles and very high heels. I bought them for my boyfriend, and he tottered around wearing them with a pair of purple and grey striped loons, a shirt with a huge collar you had to put those stiffeners in, and a pink and white PVC mac. I thought he looked fantastic.

With my first grant cheque at university I bought a fabulous 'fun fur' – a white, grey and black rabbitskin coat – and a pair of beige leather knee-high lace-up boots. Wearing those, with a mini dress, I felt like a film star. Until one night when I got horribly drunk at the Thursday night dance and peed in the boots on the way home. They were never quite the same after that. I became known as 'Piss in Boots'.

Mr Fish did sharp suits, and there were chains of shops like Lord John that did men's fashion. Half of the shops in Carnaby Street were men's shops.

I went to Take Six in Wardour Street and bought a kind of waisted donkey jacket and flared trousers so big that your shoes disappeared. I used to shop at Lawrence Corner, the Army surplus place. They had the best loons in the world, proper ex-sailor's trousers that they dyed in psychedelic colours, and other bits of naval kit like square-necked shirts and sweaters.

You bought ridiculously-shaped ties, like kipper ties, because they were halfway between being a hippie and being square. You wore shirts with collars that came up almost as high as Regency collars and down to your nipples. I remember experimenting with crimson jeans

5th MARCH 1966   ONE SHILLING

petticoat
for the young and fancy free

fun-fashion
GLOW COATS

new as tomorrow
LEISUREWAYS

personalised
PERFUMES   ★ WHAT'S IN THE STARS ★

and things like that: black jeans, crimson velvet flares, pink shirts.

I outgrew my parents' image of me as the nice daughter, the educated, well-mannered girl, who some day would make some nice man a nice wife. I started to get scruffier. Baggy jeans and loose, sloppy T-shirts with no bra underneath. Straggly hair. Long skirts that

swept the ground. Dun colours. I knew that I was rebelling against looking 'pretty'. The one thing I did not want to look in those days was 'bourgeois'. To look bourgeois was the biggest sin.

Hippies

The hippie movement was from *my* generation. I desperately wanted to be one, but I never quite made it because you had to be either terribly rich or a complete drop-out. I ended up being a sort of weekend hippie, wearing long floaty things, even occasionally flowers in my hair, but going to lectures and doing the conventional thing. And always feeling slightly self-conscious about going around in hippie gear; a bit of a fraud.

We just laughed at people who took the whole hippie thing too seriously. People who dressed up in things that looked like sheets and togas, and went around claiming to have seen UFOs and saying 'oh *man!*' all the time.

In the summer of 1967 there were flowers-in-their-hair hippies in Brighton. I put on my jeans, with my black satin shirt, long silk scarves, and every single string of beads I could find. With my hair loose, I walked through Brighton.

Haight-Ashbury was a shock and a disappointment. There were no flowers, or peace, or love. This was 1968, and the streets were tatty, the people looked dead. Too many wasted addicts hanging around; kids with their eyes glazed over and their faces old.

Music

After clothes and hair, music was the defining mantra of the sixties. If our parents had been horrified by Bill Haley and Elvis Presley in the fifties, they nearly had seizures when they heard the Rolling Stones, Them, even the Beatles. And later on, music became the essential background to dope-smoking. The music was ours, not theirs. The music was everything. Although you weren't actually creating the music, there was an incredible feeling of ownership.

I kept a list of my favourite records, starting in September 1959 with 'My Wish Come True' by Elvis Presley, followed by 'Three Bells' by The Browns and 'Keep it Up' by Dee Clark. The idea was to compile my top 1,000, but although I did keep it up diligently for years I only ever got to number 970, which was 'Somewhere in the Night' by Brian Hyland, listed in May 1963. I still have the yellowing pages, more sticky tape than paper, but still legible.

I used to buy singles in the very early sixties, when I could afford them. Michael Holiday, Tommy Steele. I remember a friend suggesting I go to Woolworth's and buy a cover version, Embassy Records, half the price of the real thing, and you just didn't do that. If I wanted Ruby Murray I wanted the *real* Ruby Murray.

MAUREEN CLEAVE

Journalist Maureen Cleave wrote a column in the Evening Standard *in the early 1960s which introduced all the new pop stars.*

"My column was called (oh shame) 'Disc Date', when the *Standard* was one of the first papers to print stories about what was still in inverted commas everywhere else – 'pop' music, as distinct from real music which was made by Perry Como.

I remember Tommy Steele telling me that until he was famous he had never been to the West End, even though the bus that ran outside his home in Bermondsey said 'Piccadilly'. Terence Stamp, who'd earned a fortune as a lorry driver since the age of 17, complained to me in 1963 that there was nothing to spend money on, nowhere to go, nothing to do. 'Nowhere to take girls, nowhere to sit down in England. But the working classes are banging on a door that's no longer closed. People like me, we're moderns. We work hard and we play hard. We have no class and no prejudice. We're the new swinging Englishmen.' Prophetic words. A week later I interviewed the Beatles. They were, I said, a vocal instrument group whose physical appearance inspired frenzy. Their haircuts I described as French. 'The only thing I'm afraid of,' said John Lennon, 'is growing old. They get old and they've missed it somehow.' Henceforth we had a youth culture."

...DAYS I'LL REMEMBER...

I was brought up to think that pop was vulgar; well, of course, vulgar was our culture, so I liked Adam Faith, and Gerry and the Pacemakers.

At school, there was a cachet about liking and having really obscure blues records. I'd seek out records by people like Blind Lemon Jefferson and Big Bill Broonzy of course, but also recordings made by the Lomax brothers of songs of the workers, recorded in the factories, songs of railway workers and hobos.

My parents bought me a Dansette record player when I was sixteen, and I left the arm off to play the latest 45 hit over and over again at full volume. They hardly ever complained, so I'm now very lenient with my own children when they play music loudly.

We didn't have sound systems in the early sixties like we have now. You were lucky if there was a record player in the house. Then, when we all really got into rock music, stereos became cult status items, especially among blokes: who had the biggest speakers, the most expensive turntable, the most records.

When I went to Oxford in 1963 there were a couple of American Rhodes scholars down the corridor, both I thought fantastically sophisticated, talking about jazz and playing Frank Sinatra loudly. That was just about the coolest thing going.

I had an almost total obsession with pop music. I would play records all the time. You'd go and buy a record – a little 45 rpm, maybe one a fortnight – and you'd just play it over and over. 'Halfway to Paradise', things like that.

Second-hand record shops started selling ex-juke-box records; instead of paying 6/10d a record, you could get one for a shilling. They had no middle, and they were all unbelievably warped, but if you could put up with that it meant that you could have loads of records every week.

I liked mod music, bands like The Who, and rhythm and blues. But I also liked jazz. Jazz was big around Hampstead, both traditional and modern, and we had a jazz club at Wood Green every Sunday. It was only half a crown or something. Some of the jazz bands turned into rhythm and blues bands later on, such as Mike Cotton. Eric Clapton used to come along regularly, with John Mayall, to the Tuesday night rhythm and blues nights.

The coming of the Beatles

I had this ridiculous feeling of superiority about the Beatles. My brother went to university in Liverpool in 1961, and he began writing home about a group he used to see called the Beatles in a club called the Cavern, and I told my schoolfriends about it. So when they made a record, I could have this pretence of knowing all about it, because I'd heard of them first. I really had street cred about that.

One afternoon in late November 1962, my friend and I used the fog as an excuse to rush home and skip the hellish after-school ballroom dancing class with the local boys' grammar school because there was a new group going to be on TV for the first time. Somebody, the day before, had brought their single into school. It was

'Love Me Do', they were the Beatles, and we were ready to break out – with their help.

When the Beatles first came out singing 'Love Me Do', I thought they were a barber shop quartet. They sounded like the Mike Samms Singers or somebody like that. I couldn't believe it when they became so popular.

I thought the Beatles were light years ahead of everyone else, and I think they changed the world.

I remember *Revolver* coming out, and we all took it very seriously: it wasn't just the Beatles doing their thing, it was educated parents sitting down and talking about it with us, and giving us the notion that what we did was important. Then *The Times* did that piece on the Beatles, and all the other groups paled into insignificance.

Everybody wanted to be Liverpudlian. I was from Birmingham, and we missed out completely in the pop music stakes. Steve Winwood was the only Brummie who made the scene, just about. Whenever I visited my friend in Liverpool it was like going to Mecca.

Dylan

I remember walking down a street in Soho one lunch hour and hearing 'The Times They Are A-'Changin' coming out of a record shop, and literally stopping in the street, transfixed. Then I went into the shop and asked if I could listen to it, which you could in those days, in a little booth. And I thought, 'Wow!' I bought it and took it home and listened to it endlessly in my bedsit, and was totally blown away.

I *loved* Dylan. I didn't understand half the words to his songs (it was years before I realized he was singing 'that's not where it's at' on 'Positively Fourth Street'), but that didn't matter. He was so strange, so cerebral, so different from all the pop stuff. Bohemian and interesting and *deep*.

It was the beginning of message songs. You actually had to listen to the words, because they were all saying something.

'Like a Rolling Stone' seemed to be Bob Dylan's message to nice bourgeois girls desperate to get out. We sat in my bedroom, half a dozen girls who'd come through the grammar school mill, and Dylan's song had a powerful effect. Creating that feeling of independence, of wanting to fly like a bird. Now it was time to leave home.

Psychedelia

Some of that 'psychedelic' music practically gave you a high without any illegal substances being involved at all. A sort of op art for the brain.

A friend used to really get into Pink Floyd's 'Set the Controls for the Heart of the Sun' when he was stoned. He'd lie there, eyes closed, and shout 'Fire retros!' just before the climax.

I remember my older sister coming home with a poster of Che Guevara, then a poster of Eric Clapton from Cream. Listening to her records of the Who. The first record I bought was 'Substitute' from Boots the Chemist; you could go to the chemist and buy all these covers of popular songs by other people.

HUNTER DAVIES

Hunter Davies was working on the 'Atticus' column of The Sunday Times *in 1967 when he met the Beatles and became their authorized biographer.*

"The thing that sums up the sixties for me is being given a reefer by Ringo, taking it home, closing the curtains, putting the phone off the hook, lighting up. Nothing happened, so after half an hour we opened the phone, put the curtains on the hook and got back to work. At the time, you see, nothing seemed to be happening. That was just like the sixties for me. At the time, it all seemed pretty ordinary; how it was, how it would always be. Only now, looking back, do I realize it was the most extraordinary decade."

...DAYS I'LL REMEMBER...

When you were with your girlfriend, there were certain songs that were basically songs for sex. Things like 'The End' by the Doors.

My favourite of all sixties bands was Them. They were fantastic live, unlike many bands of the time. I saw them at the Astoria, Finsbury Park.

The music was suddenly much more exciting. The oldies hated it, so there must have been something good there. It's endured, hasn't it; it's stood the test of time. Still being played, and bought by young people, thirty-forty years on. Cream, Led Zeppelin, all the stuff we baby boomers were brought up on.

JOANNA LUMLEY

Joanna Lumley was a model in the sixties, before finding acting fame in 'The New Avengers' in the seventies and eternal glory as Patsy in 'Absolutely Fabulous' in the nineties.

"It was 1964. Earl's Court Road was then still two-way – a hot summer's evening, and instead of the rush hour an extraordinary silence and emptiness had descended on London, on England, on Britain. I came out of the tube station and hurried down the street to my aunt's flat, where I was staying while I did my Lucie Clayton course in modelling. No one to be seen by the flower-stall, the newspaper stand. If I sprinted I would get there in time. The nation held its breath because that evening the four Beatles, all the Fab Four, were appearing live on *Juke Box Jury*: John, Paul, George and Ringo being cool, hip, smart, lippy, charming and funny. It was very heaven to be alive."

...DAYS I'LL REMEMBER...

I bought *Cheap Thrills* as soon as it became available. Janis Joplin meant a lot to me. She knew what it meant to be a gutsy, ballsy girl, to want to do everything the boys did, and then to suffer because she wasn't feminine enough. She knew all about those pent-up feelings, about the claustrophobia that comes from a straight upbringing.

Radio

Before the broadcasting honchos cottoned on to the fact that the teenage audience was the way of the future, there was very little for us to listen to. We were stuck with our parents singing along to 'Sing Something Simple', the BBC Light Orchestra and 'The Billy Cotton Band Show'. So who can forget the thrill of tuning in to Radio Luxembourg in those rock-famished days and hearing all the pop songs we'd ever desired? Even if the reception was lousy, the songs were faded out after a minute or so, and every three nanoseconds there'd be an ad for Horace Batchelor and his infallible gambling schemes based at Keynsham, spelled K-E-Y-N-S-H-A-M, near Bristol.

We'd all take the mickey out of the Horace Batchelor ad at school, saying, 'Keynsham, I'll spell that again: T-H-A-T.'

You begged for a transistor radio for Christmas, and you sat in your room and listened to Radio Luxembourg. My parents thought it was dreadful because it was commercial and played nothing but pop music, but I loved it. It was all very exciting. Music began to dominate everything, and became a talking point for teenagers.

I remember lying in the dark, listening to Radio Luxembourg, and feeling as though I suddenly belonged to a worldwide conspiracy, a movement. People everywhere were listening to the same thing, in the same way. All of a sudden, *life* was beginning.

My first awareness of people like Cliff Richard, and the fact that there were pop songs going on, was gathered around a horrible little radio set in the House library of an English public school on Sunday afternoons, listening to *Pick of the Pops*. I especially remember it as a winter scenario, with steam on the windows and lots of little boys with boils on their faces, crowding around a hissing gas fire trying to toast their crumpets, listening to Alan Freeman.

When I was about fifteen I bought myself a tape recorder, but of course I had to record off this big old radio we had, sticking a microphone in front of it. I've got loads of recordings with a canary singing its heart out in the background.

The pirate stations were such a relief because they played the same stuff as Radio Luxembourg but seemed to have a much better broadcasting facility. So for the first time you could actually hear the music properly. The whole business of them being outlawed and hounded was ludicrous; I mean, what were they doing that was so heinous? It was an early instance of 'Big Brother' meddling in *our* affairs.

Pirate radio stations were so important. We just had to listen to Radio Caroline, it was so different from everything else that had ever been on the radio. The music they played was fantastic, the DJs were fantastic, including Kenny Everett. The blurb between the records was really good. I remember lying on a rug in the garden listening to Radio Caroline on a little transistor radio and revising my History A-level notes with my friend.

Concerts

A few of us girls went to the Beatles concert in Cheltenham and they got us all screaming. I don't remember much about the concert, just the noise. Everyone screamed. It was rather like being on the Big Wheel. When that goes hurtling down, out of control, you have to scream to release yourself. Screaming, hysteria, knicker wetting – they're all related.

I remember queuing up to see the Searchers at my local town hall, but I didn't really like going to concerts because everybody screamed. It was the most mindless thing. You couldn't hear the music, and you just got deafened. So I stuck to my record collection.

I went to the Beatles concert at the Wigan Ritz, with Gene Pitney and Mary Wells also on the bill. I wore a pencil-slim skirt and I spent the whole time

TUNE IN TO
petticoat
CLUB

RADIO CAROLINE...

on Saturday at 12.45-1 p.m.,

RADIO LONDON...

on Saturday at 11.45 a.m.-12 noon.

screaming. I have no idea what they sang, but I remember the camaraderie of everyone there. We were all so happy to be there, part of a huge party.

I was sitting close to the front at the Beatles concert in Hull, and I never heard a single note. It was a continuous, deafening cacophony of screaming. To keep up that very high-pitched and very loud screaming for that long – it was well over an hour – is amazing. If you really fixed your eyes on the stage, you thought you knew which one was singing. I was obsessed with the Beatles so I was very disappointed by this concert, because I'd really like to have heard them.

When I was seventeen, in 1964, my friend and I got tickets to the Mad Mod Ball at Wembley where the Stones were playing, stuck out on a platform in the centre of the

★

THE

BEATLES

★

WINTER
GARDENS
MARGATE

★

Programme Sixpence

stadium. We had dancing tickets, which meant we could get really close. I doubt if the Stones ever played so near their audience again. I can remember their terrified faces, when they were trying to get off the stage, surrounded by the heaving, maniacal, screaming mob.

The sixties began for me when I discovered the Rolling Stones. I hated the teachers at school, I hated

BOOKENDS/SIMON & GARFUNKEL

the most bizarre event. It was just after Brian Jones had died, and the thing that sticks out in my memory is Mick Jagger opening up the box of butterflies after reading the Shelley poem 'Adonais'. The butterflies had been kept in the box too long. They flew up six or seven feet above the stage, then the Stones went into their next song – which I think was '(I Can't Get No) Satisfaction' – and suddenly the butterflies all fluttered back down to the stage. They sat there quivering as Mick Jagger stomped around the stage, stomping all over these butterflies.

authority, so when the Rolling Stones appeared on the scene I was immediately attracted. I went to see them before they were famous, at Sophia Gardens in Cardiff in about 1964, just as they released 'Not Fade Away'. It was a dance hall, rather than a concert in a theatre. You could dance away and look up at Mick Jagger's knickers on the stage next to you, practically.

We went to the Simon and Garfunkel concert in Manchester in 1968, and I remember thinking it was just like listening to the records. They were phenomenal, better than the best group around.

A friend told me one day in 1969 that there was a gig coming up the following Sunday, and they needed extra stage crew, so I said I'd do it. And it was the big rock concert in Hyde Park, the Stones in the Park concert. So we did stage management there, and it was

Dance halls and clubs

The dances were so important. We used to go to the Embassy Ballroom in Wigan, which was huge, or to Bolton Palais. I got ten bob a week pocket money, and I had to buy a pair of stockings every week because they always laddered. Then you had to pay to get into the ballroom, get a drink of lemonade in there, and your bus fare there and back. That took care of the ten bob.

My main recollection of the Cavern is an absolutely unbelievable level of noise, and a strong smell of disinfectant. Every night they swabbed it out. But there were lots of clubs around Birkenhead then, with amazing people playing, not just the Beatles: Gerry and the Pacemakers, Billy J. Kramer. They'd play the local church halls, school dances and stuff.

Rory Storm and the Hurricanes; Wayne Fontana. Great music.

I used to go to all the mod music venues, I'd ride my Vespa to the Marquee Club up West

and to the Con Hall at Finchley. I wore Hush Puppies and PVC macs. I even wore a pork-pie hat for a while, it was my dad's. Discomfort didn't seem to matter. We'd go into these dance halls wearing parkas – army surplus stuff designed to keep people warm in the frozen wastes of Antarctica, and we'd wear them in rooms full of people. We wouldn't take them off, either.

Ronnie Scott's first club was a tiny place below a Chinese restaurant, down a fire staircase. It was very grungy, but it was a jazz club, with very exciting music: a tenor player called Tubby Hayes, a trumpet player called Jimmy Ducat, a keyboard player called Georgie Fame. Ronnie Scott had a

VALERIE GROVE

Valerie Grove started her Fleet Street career as a reporter on the Londoner's Diary of the Evening Standard *in the flower-power summer of 1967.*

"The first inkling I'd had that times were really changing was at school when Mr Oliver, the economics master, seized my copy of *Private Eye* – it was issue number 4, in 1962 – with Hugh Gaitskell on the cover, and after protesting 'How cruel to poor Mr Gaitskell!' he then read the whole thing through, sniggering and chortling. So satirizing politicians was OK! Then in 1966 the first Brook Advisory Clinic opened, including one in Cambridge. So going on the Pill was not just OK for students: it was almost obligatory. And in the summer of 1967, I was on the 'Londoner's Diary' and almost every day in London there was a happening or a love-in to cover. I sat at the feet of all four Beatles at the Hilton Hotel on the hot August night when they went to hear the Maharishi for the first time. And a bunch of Sloaney young things went and squatted in a grand old house once lived in by King George VI, at 144 Piccadilly. When I met these Arabellas and Jonathans and found that even they were calling this place 'a great crash-pad' I knew Bob Dylan was right, the sons and daughters were beyond their parents' commands. And I remember great swathes of colour: Indian caftans, mirror sequins and psychedelic prints, flower-power trouser suits and all the phantasmagoria of exuberantly coloured cottons and lace and seersucker. There has never been such a colourful world, before or since."

...DAYS I'LL REMEMBER...

somewhat black sense of humour. He must have started on an absolute shoestring; I remember being there on nights when there'd be five or six other people – until midnight,

when all the other musicians would finish their gigs and come over to Ronnie Scott's.

Folk was a big thing in the early sixties, but I didn't get involved in it myself. It was all a bit too earnest; they were too purist. They were the people who booed Dylan when he went electric.

I went to the UFO club in London, in Tottenham Court Road, where Soft Machine, Purple Gang, Pink Floyd played. I used to go with my older sister. Two groovy girls from my school used to go too, and when they saw me there my status shot up. I hadn't a clue what was going on there. I remember the smell of the place, the joss sticks; and there were a lot of pills around, not so much marijuana.

COMPLIMENTARY TICKET

LA PREMIÈRE DISCOTHEQUE FRANÇAISE
CARTE COMPLIMENTAIRE - FREIKARTE
COMPLENENTARIO DILLETE
BILIEPPO DI COMPLINTI

THE PURPLE PUSSYCAT

LONDON'S SWINGIEST DISCOTHEQUE

307 FINCHLEY ROAD N.W.3
ENTRANCE IN LITHOS ROAD

OPEN FROM EIGHT TILL LATE

Telephone: SWI 2801 and SWI 325

I went to the Arts Lab once but nothing happened. I thought, is this the counter-culture? And actually, it was.

London was having a ball in those years. There was a guy called Jim Haynes who ran the Arts Lab; leading liberationist of his day. He was wonderful fun. I used to go to the Arts Lab all the time. We didn't do very much; we lay around on mattresses and watched light shows and listened to strange music and felt incredibly psychedelic. We didn't drink much, and there were only modest amounts of drugs going on. We just lay about in heaps and thought it was the coolest thing in the world.

Fundraising concerts at the Roundhouse were always really good. And there was a club in Wardour Street where I first heard a band called King Crimson. Astonishing noise, strobe lights, mind-altering substances: it took me a while to recover. It was my first experience of that type of thing.

The Saturday night dances at the Student Union seemed to attract people like Manfred Mann, the Searchers, the Hollies; all the top groups came, we took it for granted. I'll never forget Jimi Hendrix. We got into the hall and it was so jam packed there was no room for a single extra body. We pushed our way along the back wall and eventually climbed on to a windowsill and stood there. On the other side was a three-storey drop. There was a waterfall coming down the wall from all the condensation, and all you could see in front of you was this sea of humanity. Then Hendrix came on, and you hadn't got a clue what he was singing or playing because there was just this *staggering* volume of noise, totally distorted. The loudest noise I've ever heard in my life.

The Animals came and played at one of our college balls. They were appallingly young and spotty, but nevertheless they looked far wilder and more mature and interesting than we all felt in our dinner jackets. Long John Baldry played at one ball; Francois Hardie sang at another.

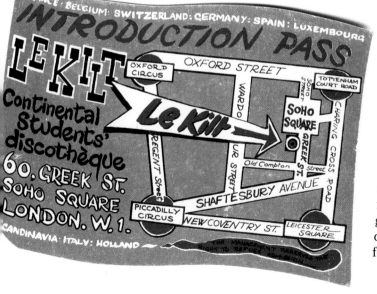

Dancing

When the Liverpool sound was starting to happen, there was a lot of local energy around. Tennis clubs and church socials had a huge number of bands to call on, really good bands. It was great music to dance to. We were being taught foxtrots and waltzes at dancing lessons, but when we went to the dances it was completely different.

When it came out, the Twist was such an innovation. You knew you looked good doing it, and you knew your parents looked bloody stupid. They hadn't been able to jive, that was too energetic, but anyone could do the twist. But only we teenagers looked good.

I remember when 'Can't Buy Me Love' came out. We did our own jump jive. We used to jump ourselves silly. I remember, too, winning a competition for the Shake. I won a pound. We had so much energy.

We did The March of the Mods, with everybody in a line doing a set dance. Joe Loss and His Orchestra. The dance floor was sprung, and it would go up and down as we danced, very simple steps like the Shadows did.

There was a great, arm-twisting, gyrating style of dancing that came in with the Tamla Motown sound. We all did it, around 1966-67. Even guys who'd never danced before found they could do it, because it meshed so well with the music. The sound

and the movement were perfect together. And even better: you didn't need a partner. For the first time, you could just get out there on the dance floor and do your thing. End of wallflowers!

Television

I vividly remember slouching around in my parents' living room one boring Saturday afternoon when the very first *Dr Who* came on the TV – listening to that eerie theme music for the first time and getting goosebumps, and being mesmerized by the amazing idea of the Tardis and its journeyings. There were other great sci-fi programmes: *The Twilight Zone* and of course *Star Trek*.

My friend Elaine used to come round to my house on Saturday night and if we didn't have anything else planned we'd watch *Rawhide* on television with my mother. We watched a hell of a lot of *Rawhide*.

6.5 Special was still around at the beginning of the sixties. And *Juke Box Jury*. David Jacobs in the chair, and Pete Murray. In early 1960 Gracie Fields came out of retirement and recorded 'Jerusalem'. They played it on *Juke Box Jury*, and they had Gracie in that booth behind the panel, so the panellists couldn't see her. And of course they all said what an embarrassment it was; then she came out and they all had to smile gracefully and shake her hand.

I can remember my grandmother watching all the banal quiz shows, *Double Your Money, Take Your Pick*, and getting really involved. If somebody opened the box and it was a booby prize and she had been shouting at them to take the money, she would just go wild, crying 'I *knew* it was a booby!' She'd have a hankie stuffed in her mouth, she was so wound up.

I used to go for my school holidays to an aunt who lived in Weston-Super-Mare and ran a rigid sort of household, where the nearest we came to listening to popular music was *Music While You Work*. But at least there we had television, and as soon as *Ready, Steady, Go* and *Juke Box Jury* started I would get a little glimpse of what was happening. But the television for them served much more as sitting down with trolleys loaded with cheese and pickles and celery sticks to watch *Armchair Theatre*, which was absolutely wonderful drama. You remember them with absolute pleasure, and wonder why they don't happen now – I suppose because we're all too impatient, we've all seen too many zippy movies.

There were some great comedy shows. *Steptoe and Son, Hancock's Half-Hour, Morecambe and Wise*. And do you remember when every comedian had to have a catchphrase? Norman Vaughan with 'swingin'!' and 'dodgy', accompanied by thumbs up or thumbs down.

Cathy McGowan and *Ready, Steady, Go* were magic, compulsory viewing. Manfred Mann singing '5, 4, 3, 2, 1' was the theme music. I'll never forget that wonderful catch-cry 'The weekend starts here!', with the accompanying feeling of freedom, excitement and *youth*.

I didn't finish work in Tottenham until half-past five, and *Ready, Steady, Go* came on at six. It was incredibly tight for me to get back to Highgate in time to watch it, but I wasn't worth living with if I missed it. I remember one Friday night when the bus was caught in some traffic snarl-up in Crouch End, and I ran all the way home in four-minute-mile time, arriving, covered in sweat, just in time to crash into the front room as the show started. My parents thought I was crazy.

When I got to university in 1966 there was a television room in the basement of my hall of residence. I very much wanted to watch *Top of the Pops* and *Dr Who* but had a suspicion this would be regarded as desperately uncool. So that first week I didn't tell anyone where I was going and snuck quietly down the stairs to watch *Top of the Pops*. My progress was halted halfway

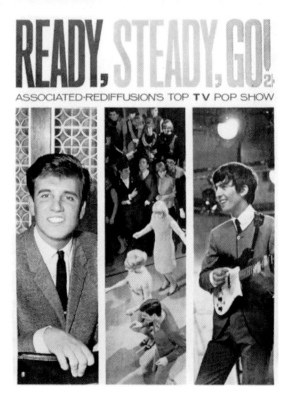

READY, STEADY, GO!
ASSOCIATED-REDIFFUSION'S TOP **TV** POP SHOW

ready steady goes live! with CATHY McGOWAN

by the seething mass of humanity gathered to do just that. I learnt that you had to arrive at least half an hour earlier to guarantee a seat. Same with *Dr Who*, same with *Star Trek*. It was such a relief. In fact they were highlights of the week, all the more enjoyable because you were watching them with a couple of hundred others, shouting and whistling and groaning in unison. Not stuck in your parents' living room with only siblings for company and a big Disapproval vibe coming from elsewhere in the house.

Glamorous programmes like *The Avengers* came along, and bizarre stuff like *The Prisoner*. And great police dramas like *Z Cars*.

John Berger did a fantastic series called *Looking at Paintings*, where he got very ordinary people, people like my mum, on the telly to talk about a Rembrandt or something. It was watched by millions, and nobody thought 'this is above us' at all. It was the same with things like *Armchair Theatre*. There was no dumbing down. They did the whole of *The Age of Kings*, which we all watched.

We didn't get colour television until the late sixties. The main impact was on televized football games: at last, you could tell which team was which.

Films, theatre, happenings

The quintessential movie about the sixties, the one that's about being inside and outside – and I felt all the way through the sixties that I was on the outside, but too close to the inside – was Antonioni's *Blow-Up*. I saw it one day and went back to see it again the next; it was *exactly* right.

I remember thinking how funny *Billy Liar* was when I read it at school. The film is one of my all-time favourites. Everybody was in love with Julie Christie. It painted a true picture of what life still really was like in the sixties. There still was an Establishment.

I've never felt comfortable watching something risqué with someone I think is going to disapprove. So I was always desperate to get my parents to bed so I could really enjoy *That Was The Week That Was*. If they stayed up I was excruciatingly embarrassed because on *TW3* they would do things like swear, which was terribly unusual then. It fitted my feelings and views; I didn't know about satire then, but its targets were the old fuddy-duddies I hated and I thought it was so funny. It was totally new, and a great experience – as long as you got your mum and dad to bed first.

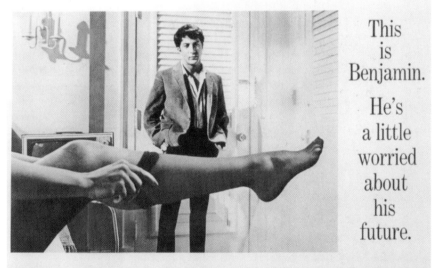

My first date with my future husband was going to a double bill of *A Taste of Honey* and *Saturday Night and Sunday Morning*. Great stuff. To our shock, when we emerged from the Raynes Park Rialto, his parents were coming out too. All the kitchen sink stuff was wonderful.

There was a sense of discovering something new that wasn't what we'd been taught. I remember thinking 'The Continentals' were really interesting; that they had something beyond Norman Wisdom and Benny Hill. They had Jean-Luc Godard.

There were only certain cinemas that you went to in the early sixties, and if it wasn't on at one of those art-house cinemas you didn't go.

Antonioni, Visconti, Alain Renais, Ingmar Bergman were all beginning to go into colour, because they'd all done black and white before and colour was for Hollywood. I remember Antonioni's first colour film was *The Red Desert* in 1964, and he was quite late. Some of those films were so violent and hideous, about the underbelly of Milano and things, but I thought they were wonderful. Oh, it's foreign, it's wonderful.

It was almost a shock when Hollywood started to make films about 'us': films like *The Graduate, Midnight Cowboy, Zabriski Point, Easy Rider.* I mean, none of us had actually hustled in Manhattan or blown up buildings in California or ridden Harleys through New Orleans, but at least these films weren't about sophisticated twenty-somethings living in swish apartments.

The Mermaid Theatre in London was revolutionary at the time: theatre in the round, theatre workshop. We used it as a launch-pad for a new range of fashion garments, and this was the first time a theatre had been used for such a thing, with music. It was an event, and made the headlines.

We went to see *Alfie* at the Mermaid Theatre, with an elderly female friend. The opening scene was a pair of knickers flying over a screen. There was an abortion scene, and the language was really confrontational. It was pretty full frontal. I asked our friend afterwards what she thought of it, and she said, 'Charming my dear, charming.' So tactful!

We went to a lot of lunchtime theatre; there were lunchtime movies at the Mermaid. There was a great artistic buzz going on. The Roundhouse put on really strange productions. One minute it would be Nicol Williamson playing demented Shakespeare; next it would be a mad French group swinging from the rafters spraying the audience with dubious liquid. There was an alarming trend in favour of hauling people out of the audience and pouring water on them or abusing them or mocking them in some way, or even taking their clothes off. 'Audience participation' happened everywhere, even in *Hair*, where you could dance on stage.

There was that feeling that we were at the cutting edge all across the cultural palette, which certainly hasn't been felt in Britain since. I'm not saying it was Berlin in the thirties, but

there was a touch of that about it. Of happenings, happening everywhere. You could be in Harrods, or standing on Victoria Station, and suddenly a whole lot of people would start shouting or screaming or ringing bells.

There was a wonderful place called the Liquid Theatre, underneath the arches at Charing Cross, which was an excuse for a group grope. You went into a labyrinth; it was a bit dark and you were blindfolded, I think, and from the second you got in there you were touched and stroked, had interesting things fed to you, and drinks, and you lay in heaps with girls and men, you weren't quite sure, who writhed on you. This blissful procedure took about half an hour, with music and bells and incense, and when you opened your eyes again you were there with all these people, some of whom were, like you, customers, and some were part of the staff. It was all very innocent but fantastically sexy and liberating, and you knew that anybody over the age of thirty would disapprove.

TONY ELLIOTT

Tony Elliott founded the listings magazine Time Out *in 1968, when he was 21.*
"I was away at school at Stowe until I escaped to London to live at home with my parents in Kensington and do my A-levels at Westminster College in 1965. It was magical because I fell in with a gang of slightly older students, bohemians rather than hippies, who knew about jazz and art movies. We'd go to see Manfred Mann at the Marquee, and the Pretty Things out at Wood Green. There was lots of fresh, New Wave contemporary culture going on – the stuff Jim Haynes was doing at the Arts Lab, Yoko Ono and her bottoms film, the Roundhouse and Underground films – that wasn't really covered in the London papers or in the desperately unhip *What's On* magazine. There was a bit in the *International Times*, but it wasn't very good. While I was at Keele University I went to the *IT* office and offered to do their listings for them, but they said no. I think I was just too young for them, and probably a bit more organized than they were. I never signed up for all that flowers and bells stuff, I was far too self-conscious even in my first hipster trousers from Carnaby Street. But in 1968 my aunt gave me £75 and I started *Time Out* – printed on a single fold-out sheet, the equivalent of eight pages. And it took off."
...DAYS I'LL REMEMBER...

Magazines and comix

1960 was the year *Mad* magazine came out in England. I remember a schoolfriend of mine's mother was a prominent actress and she'd been sent a preview copy. There was great excitement that this kind of wacky American humour, very new and very fresh, was suddenly available.

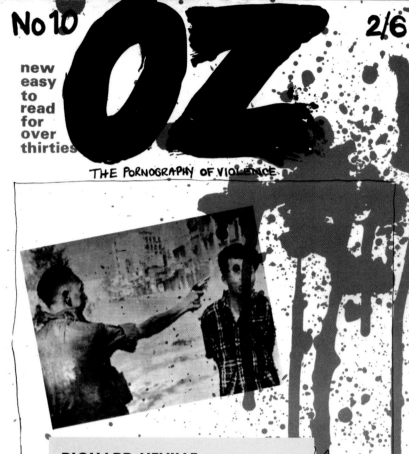

No 10   **OZ**   2/6

new
easy
to
read
for
over
thirties

THE PORNOGRAPHY OF VIOLENCE

RICHARD NEVILLE

Richard Neville was one of the founders and editors of Oz magazine.

"On sexuality, it was important in the sixties to shake out old ideas and experiment with the new and find out how fundamental things like jealousy really are. Very fundamental, as it turned out. The notion that the world would be transformed by a group grope is whacko now, but remember, the Pill seemed benign, VD was under control and AIDS hadn't been invented yet. Our stand on drugs was tame: hard bad, soft okay. I never said shoot up and have a ball. A lot of good ideas came out of the upheaval, like the end of censorship and the missionary position, the rise of ethnic tolerance, playful collaboration, ecology. We may yet be proved right about the perils of rampant consumerism."

...DAYS I'LL REMEMBER...

I was a reader of comics until very late, but I graduated in the sixties to the *New Musical Express*. Once you did that, you couldn't read the *Melody Maker*. I read every word of it when it came out on Friday, including the footnotes on the back page. I'd memorize them.

Teen magazines only began with *Honey* in 1961, and I bought it religiously from the first issue, progressing from *Girl* and *Schoolfriend*. I can remember individual issues from 1964 and 1965 because each page was devoured so carefully.

There was a wonderful women's magazine called *Nova*, I was so sad when it folded. Before that, there'd been *Honey* and *19*. The focus was on fashion, and pop music, and boyfriends. They were so exciting, and very important— more so than books, at the time.

Private Eye was compulsory reading. I remember the Christmas issues with a little plastic record, always very funny.

We had two of the great chroniclers of the sixties in Maureen Cleave and Ray Connolly writing for the *Evening Standard*.

Brushes with the world we all should have been a part of, but weren't, were one of the highlights of the sixties. Magazines made you believe this; you took your cues from them.

The *Time* cover depicting Swinging London is a defining moment of the sixties. It was also the moment we *knew* we were in the middle of something big.

Muggeridge: is he Britain's biggest bore?
ane Fonda: men I'd like to have babies by if...
Veruschka: who's zoo in modelling!

We used to call each other names after characters in the underground comics. Bobo Bolinsky – 'He's the Number One Zero. He's No Big Deal' – was a popular choice, as were the Fabulous Furry Freak Brothers, especially Fat Freddie and his cat.

RAY CONNOLLY

Ray Connolly came to London from Liverpool in the early 1960s. After graduating from the LSE he became a reporter, and later branched out to write novels and screenplays. His first film was That'll Be the Day.

"One Saturday morning in May 1963, at the height of the Profumo rumour chase, I went across to Carnaby Street, which I'd just discovered, to buy a pair of hipster trousers. It wasn't a trendy or an ugly heritaged place then, just a cottage industry in a back street made up of half a dozen little shops, but the whole place seemed to be bubbling with a kind of my-generation energy I'd never come across before.

I was with some fellow students from the LSE who were, naturally, talking endlessly about Profumo, but all I could think that morning was that everything Profumo represented appeared to belong to a different world, which had nothing to do with me, other than to amuse me.

There he was, a middle-aged politician living a sad fifties lifestyle of crumbling privilege, trapped by his own deceit, doomed by his doxy and her pal, the blonde in the little petalled hat. And meanwhile a new generation – mine – was, like a guerrilla army high on optimism, humour, satire, impudence, style and music, already scaling the ramparts and breaking into the grounds of the Establishment. It was the very cusp of change, the moment when the torch of influence was being passed."

...DAYS I'LL REMEMBER...

The Sunday colour magazines came in in the sixties, about 1964 I think. They were the first lifestyle magazines, with good journalism and photography. Photography was a key art form of the sixties. Those pictures of the Rolling Stones rolling about, Marianne Faithfull lying on her tiger rug, couldn't have come from Pathé News or television. They also showed you what you could be eating, how you could be decorating your house, where you could be travelling. They had a real knack of picking on trends, or even inventing trends, and then pushing them like hell, so that for a while we really were setting the pace for everybody, including America. It was something you measured your status by. Keeping up with the Joneses suddenly became keeping up with the Jaggers.

Books

I remember reading *The Group* by Mary McCarthy when I was about fifteen, and then a notice going out from the headmistress that people were reading 'unsuitable literature'. A lot of that went on – a lot of censorship of literature by schools and colleges.

I went through a Hemingway phase in the sixties. Then I got into Russian authors; I became aware of foreign authors. But I also discovered British women writers: Iris Murdoch, Margaret Drabble. Andrea Newman, who used to write short stories for *Honey*.

We all read Edna O'Brien's *The Girl with Green Eyes* and *Girls in their Married Bliss*. 'The book can be read,' Edna O'Brien said, 'as a cold early morning signal to young girls – don't rush into marriage.'

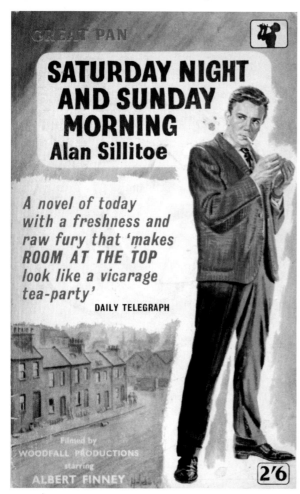

My tutor at school asked me and my friend Gareth to tea one Sunday to meet some 'interesting friends' of his. Gareth and I got to his house that day to discover that W.H. Auden and Christopher Isherwood were the other guests. It was still, then, the era when being a schoolmaster was an honourable, venerable profession: you were a distinguished man of letters, essentially.

In those hedonistic days, if you had a telephonist/receptionist they didn't have to do anything else except answer the phone and look like a dolly bird. So I read copiously. I soon got off *Passionflowers in Honolulu* or whatever, and went up to Barker's book department and saw all these books with grey covers, the Penguin classics. So I though I'd have a go at those, and the first one I picked out was *Howard's End*. And I thought this is amazing, it was just wonderful. I went through all the Penguin classics without thinking they were hard, because they weren't. They were great stories, wonderfully written.

You had to be different then, so I started to read all these French novels by people like Zola and Balzac. Although I enjoyed them, I couldn't really talk about them because no one else had read them.

The first time I really got into reading was when Pepsi Cola had a free offer. If you collected three labels off the bottles and sent them in, you got a James Bond novel. I managed to get all the James Bond novels, and we read them and read them and loved them.

My reading was very trendy during my last year of school; I read most of Balzac's novels, Chateaubriand, Flaubert, Hemingway. But I didn't get around to James Joyce. In the summer of 1965 I took the Cambridge Scholarship English paper. We'd been warned that they sometimes threw in a trick question. The whole paper was writing an

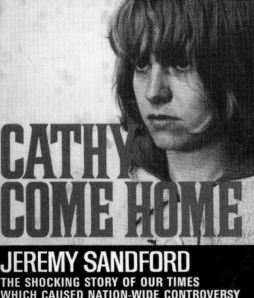

But when I finally read them they were amazing, just wonderful – at any rate, the first two books. It was the same with The *Lord of the Rings*, which I'd never read as a child. Those books alone justify the hippie philosophy.

I remember when I was in the sixth form in 1963 or so, and our English master asked if any of us had read *Catch 22*. I put my hand up, because we had it at home and I'd dipped into it, although I hadn't really understood it all that well. And I was the only one to put my hand up. So of course he asked me which bit I'd liked best, and I had to say the hospital scenes because they were the only ones I'd read. But when I did finally read it in 1966, I discovered that in fact the hospital scenes were some of the best in the book. Phew.

essay on a passage from literature. And I read the passage and thought, this is it, this is the trick question. So I wrote, basically, 'What a load of old cobblers!' And as we came out of the exam room my friend said to me, 'So, did you spot that it was a passage from *Ulysses*?'

The books *Billy Liar* and *The Loneliness of the Long-Distance Runner*, which I read when I was fifteen or sixteen, spoke louder to me than anything else.

I was interested in Kerouac and Ginsberg, although, like many a great mind of my generation, I never finished one of the books, just read a few pages to say I'd done so.

It took me a while to get around to reading the *Gormenghast* trilogy, in part because I was put off by its cult status among the more embarrassing of the ardent hippies.

Schooldaze

Secondary schools in the early sixties were still divided into public, grammar schools and secondary moderns. Children who failed the 11-plus had another chance when they took the 13-plus, but then that was it. Lots of people left school at 15: girls to serve in shops or as waitresses, or to become hairdressers; boys to take apprenticeships. Schools were run very much along the lines of our parents' days, and were pretty authoritarian and strict. But the winds of change were blowing. By mid-decade there was much more camaraderie between teachers and pupils, especially in the sixth form, and rules on school uniforms and hairstyles were being relaxed. There was a fairly traumatic time in between, however, when heads tried desperately – and vainly – to stem the tide of long hair for boys and mini skirts for girls.

daughters of gentlemen, and a lot of the girls went on to be debutantes and married chinless wonders.

I grew up in Liverpool and went to boarding school in Shropshire. We wore boaters, but it was just the local school, the kids came from the Midlands and Liverpool, shopkeepers' sons. It was probably the end of the era when ordinary people could send their children to boarding schools.

In 1960, as a thirteen-year-old schoolboy, my uniform was a pink blazer with dark grey trimmings, a pink cap, and short grey trousers.

I was sent to boarding school in 1961 and we were supposed to wear short trousers and short-sleeved shirts all year round. The uniform included six stiff white collars for shirts for Sunday wear. I never ever wore them, because that change happened just as I got there: that shift whereby traditions no longer held sway. When I arrived you had to have a cold bath every morning. The junior house was a kind of Nissen hut, and the prefects would stand in the bathroom and make sure you put your shoulders under the water. But by the beginning of my second term this tradition had been abandoned.

At the beginning of 1960 I was at a girls' boarding school in Hertfordshire. The education we got was hopeless. We got a good smattering in English and History, and that was it, that was all girls were meant to know about, then. We learnt to make conversation, to knit and to sew. It was nineteenth-century education for the

I came from a village where more or less everyone went to the local church school from age five to fourteen then left. But my mother decided that I would go to a grammar school, so when the sixties began I found myself among this new lot of people, doing unheard-of things like learning Latin.

My O-level History notebook of 1961 was identical to my brother's history notebook, which he had done five years before, because the same teacher was dictating the same set of notes. It was rote learning. I never learnt to appreciate literature, I only learnt how to tick things off and pass exams. I don't remember ever *thinking* at all.

When I was twelve, I made the decision that I would go into the commercial stream at school rather than the academic. After a year, I realized that this was utterly wrong, so I asked if I could change. And I was told no, of course you can't.

I went to a girls' high school which had none of the clubs and societies that happen now. It was straight academic. Hockey, netball and tennis were the preoccupations; nothing social was encouraged. The only time we got together with the boys' high equivalent was for a play.

My school recently had a 30th reunion of our leaving, and during the evening we were all handed a copy of a letter from the headmaster to the parents dated 1 September 1965. To me, this letter sums up the first half of the sixties. It reads:

'Dear Parents,
In my opinion, there has been a decline over the past year in the attention members of the school give to their personal appearance. It started with this matter of hair. A few senior boys began adopting long, girlish hairstyles associated with some pop singers. This seemed harmless enough, and I expected them to grow out of it. But recently younger boys, falling under their spell, have copied them, and school as a whole has an increasingly unkempt look. Quite frankly, I am tired of seeing hair creeping over coat collars and over ears, down the face, and in a few extreme cases falling over the eyes, interfering with games and physical activity. With it goes a disregard for clothes and shoes, and at times a sullen look, taken, I imagine, from the popular image of what modern young

people should look like… If your son is one of the shaggy minority, or one of those likely to copy those who are, I ask that you send him back at the beginning of next term with his hair cut reasonably short, and, with your encouragement, to take more pride in his appearance.'

Isn't that marvellous? The sixties was that time; there was a dramatic change. The generation gap was more obvious than it ever had been before.

I remember the long school photograph, with everyone at the school in it. And there was always a person who was going to run from one end of it to the other, so they could appear twice.

When I wasn't doing so well at school, it was still an age when my father thought he could fix me up to get into Oxford or Cambridge, like he'd done with my brother, but those days had gone.

In 1966 or 67, we had a strike over school uniform, and everyone turned up in their Levi's. So everyone was sent home, and came back next day in their Levi's. Eventually, the rules were changed so that the sixth formers could wear Levi's as long as they wore the rest of the uniform, including the tie.

I got beaten a few times, with a slipper or a cane.

We did some amazing things at school. We started a film club, and people like Ralph Richardson came in, Lindsay Anderson and other famous people, and they'd donate something such as a camera to the club.

In my last year of school, in 1965, there was a real feeling of – rebellion isn't quite the word; there were a lot of changes happening in the school about the treatment of boys, especially in the sixth form; there was a lot of backing off from enforcing really strict rules about dress, hair, smoking.

A girl at school who was extremely well endowed was nicknamed 'Stacks'. She also happened to be brilliant at maths, and we were all astonished at this. Girls as well as boys, we were amazed that a curvy girl could be a maths genius.

I did A-level Economic History, and I was the only girl in a class of twenty or so. I beat the pants off all of them in the mock A-level exam in 1965, and that caused major resentment. *Major* resentment.

At assembly each morning, we older girls were at the back on the side nearest the exit, and when assembly was finished we had to file out the whole length of the hall under the scrutiny of all the boys on the side opposite the exit. It was hideous; like running the gauntlet every single morning, feeling all those male eyes on you, sizing you up.

School was of course part of my everyday life but it didn't feel important at the time. Things that went on outside school were much more important: youth club, lads and dances. All the things that made you stop and think and challenge what was going on – things like *That Was The Week That Was* – happened outside of school.

I took my A-levels a year early, then spent a year doing nothing much. Nowadays you'd have a gap year, go off and do something exciting, but as it was I just hung on at school doing nothing, wasting my time. It was pathetic. And nobody suggested that I did anything else.

I went to a co-ed school, but even so there was nothing like the companionship that my own children have had in their schools. There was no friendship between the sexes then; if you made contact with a boy, it was automatically considered to be sexual. If you talked to somebody, your friends would ask, 'Are you going out with him?'

I meant to keep my school hat as a souvenir, but on our very last day of school in 1965 all our hats were collected by two girls and strung up with lots of pairs of navy-blue knickers, and hung from the school chimney.

The wonderful thing about my school was that it taught me that I could be anything, do anything. We had lots of intellectual female role models, and lots of girls went on to do science, and so on. It was a pioneering girls' grammar school and it was wonderful.

VIVE AUDACTER

Boppin' at the high school hop

We used to have senior school dances, they'd bus in the girls from boarding schools around Wiltshire and Dorset. A master and mistress would always have to start the dancing off, because all the girls were at one side of the room and all we boys at the other. A three-piece band would be hired from Bournemouth: a clarinet, someone on piano, and a drummer who sat there swishing away monotonously. They wore dinner jackets with shiny pants, and they'd play things like 'Desafinado', 'Tea for Two', and they were totally uninterested in the whole thing.

There was always a Paul Jones, and the idea was to end up with someone who looked reasonable. At my first school dance, I ended up with a girl with braces on her teeth and I took her outside and backed her into a holly bush. I met her again years later and she batted for the other side – maybe because of me.

We used to do the conventional, bog standard Christmas party at school. All games were cancelled for the month before, and you had to rehearse the Gay Gordons and the Valeta and the Military Two-Step. The best one was the one where you could

kick the person in front of you in the bum. Everybody did it, so you were flinching while you were doing it.

Extra-curricular activities

The 'school trip' was the only thing that mattered. We went over to Germany, Austria and Italy thinking that we were the best. We won the war, God was in his heaven and we were at the top of the pecking order. Big mistake. Their standard of living was so much better than ours and I realised what a con we'd all been fed by the Establishment. Everything was so much more colourful. It had a big effect on the way I viewed Britain from then on. I think that the exposure to foreign ways was one of several reasons for so much change in Britain in the sixties. It was the first time that the working classes had gone abroad without having to kill someone.

The big thing at school, apart from getting cars and taking an interest in girls, was drinking. As fifth formers, we used to go up to our local pub at lunchtime and play darts and drink beer. In those days the toilets were always outside, so one day I went out to take a leak and there were all these planks and tins and things in the way. I climbed over them, went in, and as I was standing there having a pee all the cement that formed the urinal began to disintegrate, falling and crumbling in a great big heap. I thought, bloody hell, this beer's strong, then shortly afterwards the builder came in and berated me because he was renovating and the new cement hadn't set yet.

We used to go to the pub at lunchtime, and we were too young to be served beer, but the landlord would serve us cider in the jug and bottle place, a cubicle where you could get cider as a thirteen- or fourteen-year-old.

Drinking was a huge thing at school, mainly because it was hard to get out and about at night – none of us had cars, and public transport was pathetic – so our social life revolved around drinking at lunchtime. I got a fair bit of practice in at being drunk before I went to university. The teachers would drink at lunchtime, too. Not in the same pub; we kept to separate establishments.

Beer was about 2/- a pint, and we'd get 1/6d dinner money so we'd get six of chips or three of chips and a bread roll, then you could go and get half a pint – in your school blazer. We'd go drinking at night, too, when I was fourteen, and not a very tall fourteen either. Landlords didn't seem too fussed in those days; they wanted the dough. They did stick us in the back bar, though.

Youth clubs, coffee bars and cigarettes

In the early sixties I belonged, not for religious reasons but for social reasons, to a Baptist Church Fellowship. They had socials which were totally innocuous; lemonade and cheese and biscuits.

My life revolved around the church and its social activities. It provided the youth club, friends, trips; it was a major part of my life.

It would be really unfair to be condescending about the church youth club I went to. At the time, it was great: dancing, music, records, snooker, darts, trips out, socials. At the socials we'd play games like Postman's Knock and Winking. In Winking, all the lads would stand behind a circle of chairs, and there'd be one empty chair. The person who had the empty chair could wink at any girl who was sitting on a chair in the circle, and she'd have to come and sit on his chair and give him a kiss. Winking was a great game.

The Methodist Youth Club was really important to us in the early sixties. It was terribly innocent but we had fabulous times there, just sitting about nattering or playing badminton, cards, or table tennis. We weren't interested in religion at all. Going home from the youth club was wonderful, too, because you could walk home with lads. You'd call at the chippie on the way.

In 1963 in Burton, when we should have been studying for O-levels, we began to go down to the Kavern Koffee Bar, near the bus station. It was underground and as nasty as could be. It was the nearest we could get to the real thing. Dark, hidden and dismal. It was also important that we should not have been going there.

Even in Abingdon, Oxfordshire, there was a frothy coffee café called the Mousehole, underneath the Town Hall. We would cycle in from school through the cold winter winds and sit there drinking frothy coffee and looking with indescribable envy at the Teddy boys and girls who played the juke box.

The Bis Bar in Sunderland was the first coffee bar we went to. You had to go there on a Saturday morning; anybody who was anybody went there, wearing a sheepskin jacket.

Once we started to go to coffee bars we all started to smoke. We didn't have a library at school so we were allowed out, and we'd go straight to a coffee bar and start smoking.

When I came back from a holiday in Bulgaria in 1964 I was smoking those tiny different-coloured cigarettes called Sobranie Cocktail, I think; smelly things, but I felt so cool. Gitanes were also considered really cool.

After *Breakfast at Tiffany's* there was a great vogue for very long cigarette holders. So I got one, and I'd sit there with this huge thing, in danger of lighting up other people's hair, thinking, I do look like Audrey Hepburn, I do, I do, and of course I didn't.

THE JAY TWINS

The Jay Twins, Helen and Catherine, were famous for being the long-legged blonde twin daughters of the Cabinet Minister Douglas Jay, for going to the new Sussex University (they made it the most popular university choice in 1966–7) and for wearing their Courrèges boots to a Buckingham Palace garden party.

"It all started when Max Hastings interviewed us for the 'Londoner's Diary' of the *Evening Standard* wearing our long boots from Anello & Davide. For a few years in the mid-sixties we couldn't even get on our bikes without being photographed, and written about in *Honey* and *Tatler*. Fame isn't really a good idea unless it's based on some talent, which ours wasn't – the IT girl syndrome. We weren't even dress designers, we just had the right figures and faces and our father was a government minister. At Sussex we were always being pursued by paparazzi or whisked away to some television studio to give 'the teenage angle', but the university authorities never stepped in to say it had to stop. And we were pre-drugs. We all had such a good time we didn't need drugs. I suppose we were what is now called 'famous for 15 minutes'. But it was tremendous fun and we didn't take it too seriously."

...DAYS I'LL REMEMBER...

I rolled liquorice-paper Old Holborn cigarettes for a long time; I thought that was cool. We were constantly trying to pretend that we were less respectable than we were, I think.

Virtually everyone smoked then. You not only had to remember whose round it was for drinks, you had to remember whose round it was for fags. If anyone didn't buy a round or pass out the cigarettes, we thought it was outrageous.

College days

1965 neatly divides the sixties, and it changed my life totally. Before then it was church youth club, school, sport and pop music; in 1965 I went to university. Part of the change in my life was stopping all conventions when I left home, so for the first term I didn't wash or cut my hair once.

I was filthy. I didn't go to many lectures. All standards of civilized existence disappeared. Then I got home at Christmas and realized I was being ridiculous.

It was only when I went to college in 1963 that I felt I'd joined the teen-age, because before then I'd been a schoolgirl, and therefore restricted. You fantasized about freedom, and what you might be doing: listening to pop music, and going into smoky dives, and smoking. I didn't do any of that. So I was watching what was happening in the sixties from the sidelines, waiting to join in.

I didn't know anyone whose parents had been to college or university, and none of my friends did either. Yet we saw it as our right, even though we were the first generation who had such education available to us.

There was an inevitability about it all: you took your O-levels then your A-levels, then you went to university. And in fact no one from our background had ever gone to university before. But it didn't feel like a privilege or anything unusual at the time.

As a girl, going to college was all bound up with the whole Women's Lib thing. It seemed the most natural thing in the world, to go to university and compete with boys on an equal footing, yet that equality was in its infancy, really.

I had been placed in a girls' hall of residence. You were only allowed home twice a term, and you had to be in by half past ten every night unless you asked for a late pass. And yet we were right next door to a newly built co-ed 'student village' where people had total freedom. I had had more freedom at home than I had in college.

At ten o'clock every Saturday morning you had to go up to the dining hall in my hall of residence to collect your supplies for the weekend. These usually consisted of two eggs, a tin of curried beans, three slices of bread and an apple. Stupid stuff. I was horrified to discover that you were not allowed to cook onions because they made a smell. It was part of the written rules. You weren't allowed to wear rollers in public parts of the building, either.

During the week, dinner was always formal. There were long refectory tables, and a stage with high table. Every evening, certain students were invited to be guests at high table with the Warden and the moral tutors. Before that, you went into the Senior Common Room and had a glass of sherry. This was the most awful thing I could have ever imagined. I hadn't gone to university to be part of this charade, I thought. The people you had to talk to had nothing in common with ordinary people, they lived in a different world.

JULIAN BARNES

Julian Barnes, the novelist, was still up at Oxford in the summer of love.
"The sixties didn't happen until the seventies for most people – including me. I was at Oxford from 1964 to 1968, but there were so many different circles, and flower power affected only a very small number. I didn't know anyone who went on the Grosvenor Square march. I wore my hair long, and had a pair of purple jeans which were excruciatingly uncomfortable at the crotch; but I knew only one person who ever mentioned drugs. He would refer knowingly to 'big H and little h', which years later I presumed had meant heroin and hash; but this seemed a personal eccentricity rather than an interesting fashion. I knew about LSD because I'd read my Aldous Huxley, and about opium because of Cocteau and Francoise Sagan. Anyway, sex seemed such a hallucinatory business that you didn't seem to need any further additive. Apart from that, I suppose I kept my head down, working. I suppose I was sixties-ish in not thinking in any practical terms about the future, just blithely assuming things would turn out in some pleasant but undefined way."

...DAYS I'LL REMEMBER...

In that first month at university I met everyone who is still my friend. Apart from relatives, there is no one from the first eighteen years of my life that I have anything to do with.

I didn't want to go into a hall of residence at university, so I chose digs, where you live with a family. I arrived there in October 1966 wearing my best suit, carrying my suitcase, and knocked on the door expecting a loving family to welcome me. This harridan answered and acted like some nightmare landlady. She was only in it for the money, didn't care about *me* at all, or the other seven students she had living there.

The course I was doing at Chelsea College in 1967 was terrible, but living in London as a student was wonderful: Portobello Road, pubs and clubs, buying *Private Eye*. It was a new, exciting culture.

We seemed to spend the entire three years at university either sitting in the Student Union coffee bar, shredding polystyrene cups, listening to the Spencer Davis Group and generally 'festering', as we called it, or in the Union bar, playing table football and getting drunk.

The three years of my undergraduate life – 1965 to 1968 – I still regard as the Golden Age of my life. I've had better times since as regards personal success and family life, but those three years made me what I am.

Shared houses and other domestic horrors

About a million of us shared an enormous, perishing cold old house off Palatine Road in Manchester. The water in the washbasins would freeze over regularly, so we'd all have to wash in the Student Union. We had so many parties it's a wonder the neighbours survived. After one party the living room burnt down, something to do with the wiring and the record player being left on. I lost my copy of *Sergeant Pepper* in that fire. Still rankles.

The blokes in our house didn't have a clue how to look after themselves. I mean, I didn't have much clue, but I sort of knew the basics. One guy wanted to fry an egg for breakfast one morning but couldn't find any oil or fat. So he tried to use vinegar.

With four blokes sharing a flat we had a roster for cooking, but one bloke had no idea. He put a pan of chips on one night, then after about half an hour he came into the living room and complained that the chips weren't going brown. We asked if the fat had been hot enough when he put the chips into it. 'What fat?' We went out to the kitchen and found he'd been trying to cook them in water.

People were very cavalier with other people's property, as I recollect, especially with food and records and books. I still miss my copy of Ferlinghetti's *A Coney Island of the Mind* that was taken in 1969. But some people went to absurd lengths to protect their territory, writing their names on eggs and so on.

In 1966 I shared a bedsit in Hampstead with an old schoolfriend. It had two gas meters, one in the kitchen which took shillings, and one in the bathroom which took pennies. It cost 4d to have a bath. On Saturdays we'd put money on horses, cross our fingers and hope that we'd win so we could have a good weekend. We got up early to get the milk off other people's doorsteps.

A lot of my sixties memories are really grubby. I was desperately poor. I lived for a while in a tenement in Dundee, which was grotty, dark, damp and dirty. We shared a toilet with six other tenements, and we didn't have a bathroom in the building.

Food

Our attitudes to food were pretty primitive in the early sixties. In fact, mine remained that way for most of the decade. I started by being horribly sick when taken to Spain by my parents in 1962, because I couldn't stand the taste or even the smell of garlic. I kept the momentum when I first saw my sister cooking real spaghetti in 1964: I was astonished when I saw her feeding these long, stiff strands of pasta into a pan of boiling water, because I'd only ever seen or tasted tinned spaghetti before that.

I was worse than useless about food when I left home in 1965. I had never even eaten a tomato. I got through the sixties without eating anything different from the fifties at all. I can remember going to the Plaza, Manchester's first and best Indian restaurant, and ordering sausage and chips. They had to have that sort of thing on the menu, then. That was pretty much what we lived on in the sixties: beans on toast, fried eggs, chips, things like that.

In 1966 I bought Elizabeth David's Italian cooking book, because all you could get in restaurants – affordable ones, that is – was transport caff food.

People were just starting to go out to eat. I remember the Berni Inn in Worcester, where we'd go on Friday nights to have chicken in a basket and a glass of red wine, followed by an Irish coffee. Great fun.

We used to go to an Indian restaurant where you could get half a biriani for 2/6 – a plate of rice with almost pure chilli sauce and a couple of lumps of meat. People had drunk so much by the time they got there that all they could taste was chilli. It was the first Indian food I'd had.

The first time I was taken out to a meal in a pukka restaurant was to the Ark in Kensington. It was amazing, really classy. I had a Mont Blanc pudding; it was like a mountain, with chestnut puree in the middle, then round that it had pure whipped cream, then round that was meringue. It was all new and exciting.

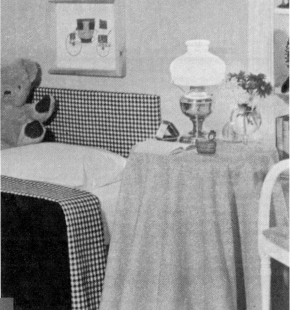

Household style

I remember getting our first telephone when we moved down to London in 1960. In those days the exchanges had names as well as numbers; ours was ARNold 3062, because all the exchanges around us were named after poets.

My Auntie Marjorie had her kitchen redone in the early sixties, mainly in orange. It even had orange spotty seats. I remember her telling us she thought it was really great, because 'it looks just like a snack bar'

Hardly any rental properties in the sixties had fridges. In summer you kept your milk in a pan of water on a shady windowsill.

I had a letterhead that read '84 St George's Square and so is the Pope'.

When I got to college in 1965 I couldn't phone home because my parents had no telephone, so they arranged to go to the local telephone box to call me at certain times each week.

CONTINUED FROM PAGE 100

HARRY'S ROOM

Victorian hatstand (on fourth wall, not shown)—in whirly bentwood, 6 ft. high. Can be found in antique markets, sales, etc. Strip with Polycel before painting a bright colour and drape with anything from coats to handbags. (Price about £5)

Wardrobes basic whitewood in the Liden range. From Maples (price £6 approx., depending on size). Painted in gloss for shiny effect, with drawer fronts, panels and top covered with Sanderson's fabric (Alhambra Range ZH 209/4, price 20s. 9d. yd.).

Chair finished in white stove enamel. From Maples (No. VL/VL. Price

it's your move

ROSY'S ROOM

Lampshade enormous spherical shape in paper. From a selection at Maples.

Coffee-pot big-brew enamel pot. Selection of brightly-coloured ones available from shops and stores throughout country.

Spotlight fitted to wall for additional light on mirror and sleeping area. From a selection at Maples.

The house had that décor that was a mix of classic eighteenth century Enlightenment and very pop, Baltic pine stuff. A great stash of vodka in the cellar, too. And we'd sit there and it felt that, vicariously, we were really in the thick of Swinging London.

All the new sixties furniture styles, Heals and Habitat and suchlike, were borrowed from Scandinavia. 'Isn't it good,' etc.

When I left home to go to university in 1966, I bought myself a portable record player for about £20 and a fake-fur, purple-backed cushion. I thought they were the height of chic. I bought myself a Joan Baez record, a Dylan and a Beatles, and I was all set.

We all had to have collages on our walls, pictures made of images torn or cut from magazines. I had one featuring the gorgeous model Veruschka, and lots of photos from *Honey*.

Friends moved down to London in the late sixties and got a flat in Holland Park. They painted all the walls dark purple, which I thought was so cool. You couldn't see a thing, but it was cool.

We only really became aware of interior décor at the end of the sixties, because until then it had been either fifties-style parental homes or student grot. Then everything had to be purple or black, or midnight blue.

In 1966 some friends of mine were house-sitting Peter and Wendy Cook's house in Church Row in Hampstead. They had a life-size model of Spotty Muldoon in the bedroom; you could press the stomach and it had a tape recorder inside going 'Hello, I'm Spotty Muldoon' in that famous voice.

Behaving badly

Of course we behaved badly. In the fifties, when teenagers were invented, they turned into Teddy boys and were really threatening. Mods and Rockers were renowned for bank holiday, seaside battles. We were less violent, but just as likely to get stuck into the booze. And we had something entirely new, to which some of us took with a vengeance: recreational drugs.

Booze

The first getting drunk was when I was about fourteen. I'd gone round to my friend's on my bike, and she'd got some bottles of Babycham. I must have had two bottles, and I couldn't get back on to my bike to ride home. I thought, 'Ooh, this is a really strange feeling.' I had to walk home.

We went to the local ballroom and a woman was on stage singing 'Climb Every Mountain'. We all joined in and I did my usual drunken thing of singing 20 octaves higher than everyone else. For some reason we went back the following night, and there was a request for members of the audience not to sing along with the act.

I had four older sisters, who had bottle parties in the early sixties – a hangover from the fifties. They lived on the top floor of our house, and their friends would come and bring a bottle and hand it to the barman, which was me, even though I was barely into my teens. So I discovered my love of alcohol early.

I first got drunk in 1964, when I was seventeen. Friends of my parents held a goldfish warming party, and they just kept filling my champagne glass. I ended up with the whirling pits, being sick in the bathroom for hours. It should have put me off booze forever, but alas it didn't.

We went up to London for the weekend during my first term at university and went straight out on the piss. I got legless, and fell over and gashed my head on the way back to the hotel. Blood everywhere. In the hotel room I collapsed on the floor and

. . . and no wine ever had a lovelier birthplace

The Palace of Mateus, Douro, Northern Portugal

Photograph by Percy Hennell

MATEUS ROSÉ

the enchanting pink wine

passed out. When I woke up I couldn't move. I panicked and thought I was paralysed, until I realized that my face was stuck firmly to the carpet with congealed blood.

When I was about fifteen I went to a really posh Chinese restaurant with my best friend and his family. Mr Hong's, I think it was, in London. I'd never eaten this type of food before, and, coupled with the red wine, it was too much for me. They dimmed the lights in the restaurant to sing 'Happy Birthday to You' to my friend and I fell arse over tit off my seat and slid underneath the next table, which was occupied by Lulu and one of the Gibb brothers (the Bee Gees).

Pubs were such a social scene. My father took me to my local, the Nag's Head, for the first time, when I was about seventeen. I certainly wasn't eighteen.

My father used to try to stuff us with gin and pastis. He thought that at any age you should be able to hold your liquor like a man, so we had to start early. He's now in his nineties and going strong.

I started going to staircase parties – parties held on staircases in the halls of residence at university – where you took a bottle of cheap cider or wine as your entrance ticket. They were terrific parties. They usually ended up with everyone being sick all over the stairs as they went out.

At sixteen I moved into a flat in Putney with a friend; you could do that, then. It was like moving to Hollywood or something. We did incredibly innocent, wild things, like get dressed up in long skirts, weird make-up and military jackets, and get drunk and have dinner in the flat, just the two of us. The corner shop sold bottles of wine for 7/4d, and it was absolutely awful stuff. We bought lots of it, and drank ourselves stupid.

ROBERT LACEY

Robert Lacey is the biographer of the Queen and Princess Grace and co-author of The Year 1000.

"I started off the sixties as a prefect wearing a school cap. Then I did Voluntary Service in Africa in long khaki shorts and knee-high socks. When I left university in 1967 the uniform was still cavalry twills and Hush Puppies. The caftans and beads that the Beatles wore were a sort of fancy dress you might put on if you went to a pop festival. As I remember it, the sixties didn't really permeate ordinary life until they were nearly over. But then I came to London, got myself a Beatles jacket, grew my hair – and never looked back."

...DAYS I'LL REMEMBER...

We had a huge party in our shared house, during which the toilet became completely blocked. It was a really revolting scene. The next morning we found one member of the household trying to clear the blockage with a saucepan.

A bunch of us students used to meet in a pub most weekends, and some of the regulars bitterly resented us. One particular old biddy would sit there shaking her fist at us and shouting, 'It's our taxes that pay for you louts!' I used to dream of coming across her on a zebra crossing and running her down. But in retrospect, she was right. She was paying for our grants, and our behaviour was pretty awful.

In our final year of university, in the late sixties, we developed the habit of pouring pints of beer over each other's heads. We thought it was great fun, but it got out of hand sometimes when the person the beer was being chucked at ducked and the innocent person at the next table copped the lot. Occasionally it got really out of hand, and there were fights, or threats of violence.

Made for each other.

We went to the pub every single night. That's all we wanted to do: be adult enough to knock it back every night. We'd pour appalling stuff down our gullets, bull's blood. And Watney's Red Barrel was the only beer. Shocking stuff. All the good beer had disappeared, and the campaign for real ale hadn't started.

We'd have a bottle of gin between us all before we hit the nightclubs. If I had six gins I was sick, then I was all right.

Most of my bad behaviour was getting drunk. I seem to have been totally drunk for about fifteen years. I never saw certain people sober for years – including my future husband. We used to drink filthy stuff like giant bottles of Hirondelle wine and Party Sevens, and Number Four and London Pride sherry. You'd wake up in the morning not daring to open your eyes, wondering what it was going to be like.

I was always rather pleased it was all happening, but also always slightly tense, especially if we were doing something wrong. It was all wonderful, but I was never quite at ease when we were in pubs chanting obscenities or smashing glasses.

Most of the fights I saw in the sixties were really vicious, and over stupid things like someone spilling beer over someone's suede shoes. Glasses and bottles would be broken, and shoved into people's faces. It's much more civilized now, pubs are more civilized.

Those days seemed far safer. The word 'mugging' may have been in use in America, but it wasn't in England. In 1969 I lived in Moss Side in Manchester, and our landlord was West Indian. I used to go to a club with him after the pubs shut, and I'd be the only white guy there. I used to come out at two o'clock in the morning and walk home, and I never felt the slightest bit bothered or threatened.

We were drunk a lot – the obsession was with drinking ten pints every night. There was a men-only bar at the pub I went to in the mid-sixties; it was all sport and booze. There were no drugs at first. That was our salvation, perhaps. By the time drugs came along we'd got into the swing of drinking heavily, so when we got into dope we'd already had a skinful before starting to smoke. It kept you from being pretentious, which an awful lot of druggies could be.

Drugs

My boyfriend went up to Edinburgh University in 1964, and he rang me one night to tell me he was absolutely stoned out of his tree. I got terribly self-righteous and gave him a huge lecture about the dangers of drugs – and within a couple of years I was at university myself and hoeing merrily into whatever I could lay my hands on.

My brother-in-law was a minor drug dealer in the early sixties; one night he let me smoke some dope, even though I initially refused. He sat me down and told me all about marijuana. His advice to me was, don't take anything in a pill, just smoke dope. So I did.

One night at the J 'n' J Club – a fantastic dance club in Manchester where the sweat gathered on the ceiling and poured down like rain on the dancers – I noticed my boyfriend and a friend of his passing a cigarette between them. I told them there was no need to share as I had plenty of cigarettes – at which point, of course, it became clear that they were sharing what I then called a 'reefer'. I flew into a rage and lectured them all the way home. Eventually of course I tried it myself.

"*We have reason to believe you are carrying certain substances of a hallucinogenic nature.*"

asked me to roll a joint I couldn't have done. Except I was curious, and started smoking in the end.

I took some speed before going to a concert by Mountain at the Rainbow. Afterwards we went back to a friend's flat and smoked tincture. I had that 'If only my father could see me now!' feeling. All the middle class in me thinking, 'Ha ha ha, I'm with the druggies! I'm hitting the underground big time!' I wasn't at all, of course.

About ten of us – this was the real student life, wasn't it – would meet in a flat and put on very loud progressive rock music: Emerson, Lake and Palmer, Pink Floyd, Quintessence. Everybody would end up absolutely paralytic. I can remember being so stoned that I had to concentrate all my energies to get to the loo. And the drug squad coming to the flat and finding a packet of contraceptive pills in the dustbin.

I started taking drugs when I was about 14, in 1965, introduced to them by the older kids in my school. Money was very tight, sometimes I didn't get pocket money, but I scrounged and saved to scrape together 17/6d, and managed to buy some hashish. I spent the whole time laughing.

The first real drop-out I went out with was a guy who was part of the Liverpool 8 scene. We used to go back to people's 'pads'. I didn't know what to do, I didn't know how to go 'phew, phew, phew' – you know, inhaling deeply and noisily. If anyone had

Those early dope-smoking days were full of paranoia. We spent whole evenings twitching the curtains, convinced there were police surveillance cars parked opposite our house. And we made elaborate contingency plans for flushing the stash down the toilet in the event of a raid. Ha! I doubt the local constabulary gave us a moment's thought.

Getting stoned was fantastic in the beginning. I'd never felt such a thrill, sitting in darkened rooms with lots of other people, passing joints around and making sure I didn't bogart, listening to fabulous music by Family and Janis Joplin, Big Brother and the Holding Company, Pink Floyd, The Band, Cream, Yes, King Crimson, Love – oh, tons of wonderful stuff. And laughing, laughing so hard I thought I'd died and gone to heaven. I really miss smoking dope. I used to enjoy it enormously.

Dope was such a huge freedom thing, and a huge Us and Them barrier between us and our parents.

We used to 'score' in Moss Side. I'd drive and keep watch while the boys disappeared into dubious basement clubs, hoping they wouldn't be mugged or ripped off. We'd buy cherash, bush, Leb gold, Afghani or Paki black. Tiny amounts of hash, the size of a fingernail, for a quid or so. If it was your turn to roll the joint you had to be really careful when the block got down to the size of a pinhead. I can remember the shame and horror of being the one who lost the last piece. And frantic mornings spent combing through the hairy things you find down the backs of sofas or under the arms of chairs, trying to find the microscopic bit of hash lost the night before.

We didn't get on to acid until 1968 or so. It seemed really frightening at first; there were so many scare stories in the papers, and everyone seemed to know someone who knew someone who'd had a bad trip and ended up blind from staring at the sun, or in a loony bin. In the end we got really into it, but I always found the experience slightly disappointing, slightly contrived. You sat there and felt you ought to be experiencing all this enriching, tactile, sensuous stuff, and in reality you just felt slightly odd, jangly and jittery.

We had a wonderful time at the 'sit in' in 1969. Bands all night, lots of dope, a hall full of people grooving. I can't even remember what it was all about now, and I don't think it mattered that much at the time. The only downside was that it was freezing, and we all had to huddle together to keep warm. A couple of my friends rolled themselves in the floor mats that had been in front of the main doors – filthy mats, people had been tramping grey slush onto them all evening, but when you're stoned you don't care.

I'd never really believed the expression 'turning green' until a friend first tried dope. He didn't smoke cigarettes, but wanted to appear cool and accepted a joint one night. He turned the colour of pea soup.

For years, I didn't take any drugs. No one noticed, because it's really easy in a big group of people, nearly all stoned, just to pass on the joint without taking any yourself. But I bet my friends would have been astonished to know I didn't smoke.

The whole drug scene scared me. I think I thought, if I get into this at all, I'll get into it in a deep, deep way. And I don't like losing control. The people I knew in the drug scene were kind of scary people; criminal underground rather than alternative underground.

I had a very depressing, working-class background. But it kept my feet very firmly on the ground: I never did drugs. I used to watch people taking them; I was a great watcher and observer of what was going on. I used to watch this horrible greasy thing being passed around a group of people sitting on the floor and I'd think, ugh! Because if someone had put something in their mouth, you just didn't put it in yours. I couldn't bear the thought of someone else's spit in my mouth. I recently told someone that I never smoked dope and he said, 'But what did you do in the sixties?'

I only had one close friend who was a regular smoker of hash in those days, and he was always the object of scorn in the pub.

There was X, sitting staring vacantly in the corner of the cubicle in the union bar, and everyone would say, oh that's X, he's had a bad trip. That's all I knew about him. He never said anything. Was he a victim of the sixties? Would he have had just as bad an experience another time? We'll never know.

Even though I've never rolled a joint I thought smoking them was brilliant, because as soon as you had one you'd just sit around giggling. It was such a pleasant experience, and it seemed utterly harmless. But I did wonder if it made you lazy, because you drifted off into this nice dreamy world. Because I have this protestant ethic that anything that's enjoyable has to be suspicious, and you should spend most of your life working.

'I got you, babe': teenage romance

Until late in the decade the whole teenage romance thing was very much as it had been since time immemorial: girl meets boy, boy wants sex, girl either lets him (and loses him and/or ends up with baby) or doesn't let him (and loses him). Then along came the Pill, and a whole new world of carefree sex opened up. Except there was a price to pay eventually, of course. And mostly, women paid it.

The dating game

We were allowed a fair bit of leeway by our parents. We used to have these barbecues at a local caravan site, and wide boys from Swansea, who had Dansette record players, would come along. They had surf boards, and slicked-back hair, and they were like a different breed of animal.

My friend took me to a youth club and one of the older boys there – he was in the sixth form, while I was only fifteen – began to walk me home and we started kissing. I didn't like it at all; it seemed very wet and rather distasteful, and my mouth was all chewed to pieces.

I remember how unpleasant those early snogging sessions were, with saliva everywhere and teeth clashing and smelly breath and hideous sucking noises and a chin prickled to death by skin in need of a shave. You'd get a terrible rash later. It was all so different from what we'd been led to expect by fairytales and other romantic crap!

We used to go up a local tower and spit on the girls beneath from over the edge, like camels. The spit would go drifting down.

The worst moment of my life was finding out at school how children are conceived. Because I thought there's no way, ever, my parents could have done that! It was a real shock when I realized that there was no other way they could have done it. I was nearly sick.

When I was at school, boys were very much things to look at; creatures. We spied on them and talked about them, but we didn't interact. If you did, you were considered 'fast' and 'common'. Those girls always seemed to be having a good time, but of course they were common, and therefore despised. They had badly dyed hair, and were not expected to Get On in Life.

Our sole aim in life was meeting boys. That's what it was all about, really. Whatever you did, it was about where you could meet lads.

I thought the word 'crush' was invented for me: I was always desperately in love with someone, but it was never the person I was going out with. It was a real stigma not to have a girlfriend, so I always had one.

Funfairs were like a magnet. The rock music belting out, the Whip and the Big Dipper, the Big Wheel and the Wall of Death. They were an opportunity to meet rough lads. The minute they looked at us we were frightened to death, but it was exciting. They were greasy, horrible lads,

but there was something basically very sexy about them. They'd stand casually on the Waltzer taking your money – we'd be clinging on with both hands, and we'd think they were brilliant.

We started going to our friends' houses when their parents were out and playing Spin the Bottle and Postman's Knock. They were very innocent pursuits, but at the time they seemed like such naughty things to do.

Remember those warning lines about being frightened off when a boy starts breathing heavily, because that's when he can't stop? I used to read that in women's magazines, and imagine they'd start panting and go into some hysterical frenzy.

I was totally naïve about sexual relationships until I was about eighteen or nineteen. The first week at university, I met this girl and chatted her up – or rather, I thought I'd chatted her up, but she wandered off. The next morning I found her in my flatmate's bed.

In those days you had to wade through women's underwear. Normally, if you were lucky, it was a quick unsnap of the bra strap, panties down and you were right. But there were millions of configurations of bra straps. Every bra strap was different. You could spend half an hour trying to figure it out.

It was a nightmare wearing a pale-coloured jumper or blouse. You'd get home and just as you were walking in the front door you'd realize that the front of your jumper was covered in grubby fingermarks.

Virginity was our big problem. We still had it more or less intact in 1963. We wanted to keep it and lose it at the same time. We knew about sex, sort of knew what 'going all the way' meant. But there was a lot of mystique about virginity and we had grown up with all the talk about not losing it. It was drummed into us: Nice Girls Don't.

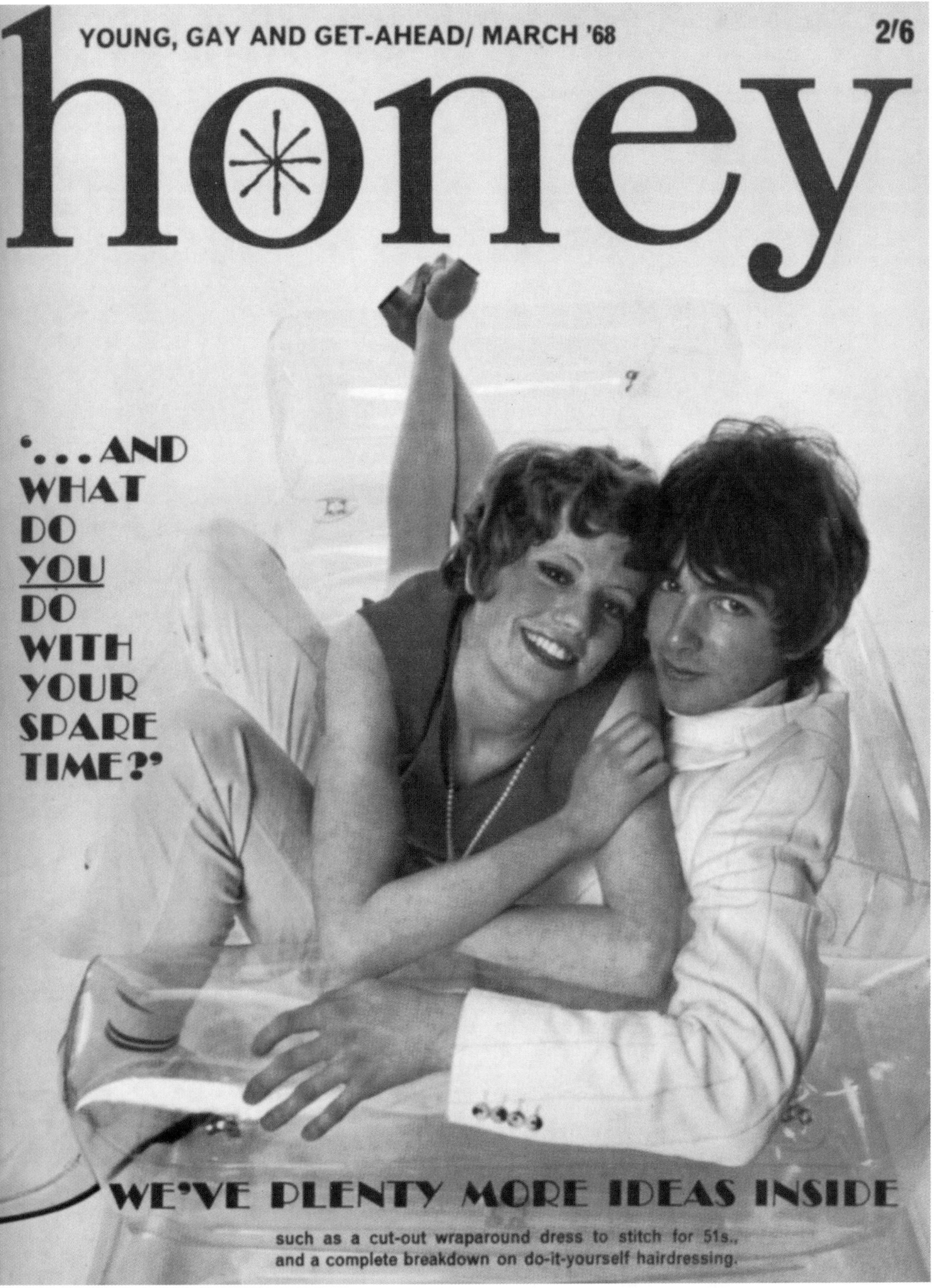

YOUNG, GAY AND GET-AHEAD/ MARCH '68
2/6
honey
'...AND WHAT DO YOU DO WITH YOUR SPARE TIME?'
WE'VE PLENTY MORE IDEAS INSIDE
such as a cut-out wraparound dress to stitch for 51s.,
and a complete breakdown on do-it-yourself hairdressing.

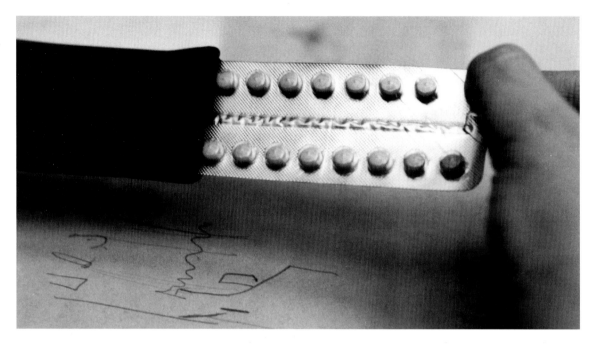

The local barber used to sell contraceptives. I was desperate to have sex, but I didn't know what to do. I couldn't buy them from him, in a small town – everybody would know. But I was terrified of getting girls pregnant, so I'd literally slept with several women before I actually had sex.

I remember going to school and saying 'Yeah, I've had sex!' to my male contemporaries—this was before any sex education was taught. I had no idea what was involved, and all I did was snog; heavy petting. The relationship lasted that one weekend, then that was that. It was mostly just misery, thinking about it and discussing it with friends. I found it very difficult to work it all out, even when they did start sex education classes.

I had a lot of failed affairs because I wasn't at all self-confident, but when the dam burst it was phenomenal. Getting emotionally involved was not good form; you had to be detached. Once I learnt that, I was very successful. Once you got over the hurdle of knowing what to do, it was pretty easy for us guys in the sixties.

A lot of the time, sex was a thing that you just looked at. There was a tremendous amount of enthusiastic snogging, but quite a lot of the girls I went out with behaved just as they would have twenty years earlier and said no, that's far enough.

When my boyfriend found out that his flatmate at university was gay he went ballistic. Kicked him out, refused to speak to him ever again, the works. It was terrible – but those attitudes were widespread. It was a brave man or woman who came out of the closet in the Swinging Sixties.

I had never heard of a homosexual, had no idea what the word meant, until I was eighteen. Then when I saw some men with umbrellas in 1965, I thought, oh, they must be homosexual. I'd never seen a man with an umbrella before. It's almost unbearable to remember my level of naïvety.

The cultural and sexual misunderstandings in those days were rampant. I had a full affair with an Italian man when I was living in Paris in 1963, who I thought was madly in love with me because he said so. He'd been back to

England with me for Christmas to meet my family, then it was summer and he was going back to Italy to see his family. So I assumed he'd invite me. And he looked at me as though I was mad, and said he couldn't possibly introduce his family to a girl whose own parents had been divorced—and while he didn't exactly say so, 'and who has also lost her virginity' was clearly implied.

'Free love'

The Pill became available to the public in 1961, but even in the late sixties its use among unmarried girls and women was frowned upon at best, seen as criminal at worst. To live together as an unmarried couple was extremely difficult outside trendy parts of London, landlords and ladies having yet to come to terms with the sexual revolution. The old morality had broken down, but nothing had come along to take its place. And we had the distinct – and probably correct – impression that the older generation didn't like us. And they especially didn't like our sexual freedom.

My thoughts were that you shouldn't really have sex until you were married; pre-marital sex was wrong. I felt very strongly about that. Although the fear of getting pregnant must have been a factor, too. But the whole free love aspect of the sixties completely passed me by.

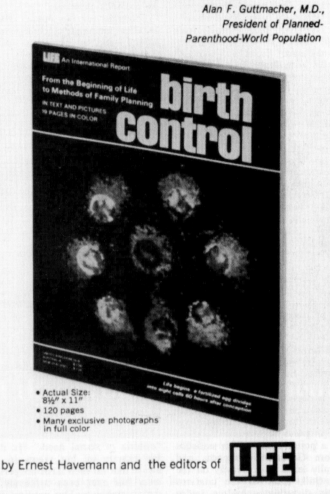

My boyfriend and I wanted to live together at university in 1967, but in Manchester in those days it was absolutely impossible. It would also have been impossible to explain to our parents. So we used to rent two places then live in one – one of us sneaking in and out of the chosen flat in the hope that no other occupants realized there was a couple living there.

My sister went to see our local GP in London when she was seventeen, in 1963. She wanted a prescription for the Pill. Instead, she got a lecture followed by the shouted admonition: 'Wait until you are married!'

It was really difficult to get on the Pill even in 1967, the height of the 'free love' era. I was at Manchester University and there wasn't a doctor within miles who would prescribe the Pill to the students. Then

word got around that an old, sympathetic doctor out at Eccles – miles away on the train – was giving out prescriptions. I trundled out there and was duly given the precious piece of paper. All of us who made the journey forever after called the Pill 'Eccles cakes'.

The worst moment about spending a night with a guy, in the early days, was waking up in the morning and knowing he'd see me without my eye make-up on. I knew he'd go off me then!

I cohabited with my boyfriend from 1966. I remember sitting my mother down and telling her that I was moving into a flat with Chris, but that we weren't going to get married, and expecting the balloon to go up. And she said, 'Oh well, you'll need some double bedding then, won't you?' and she took me out and bought me blankets and a set of sheets.

There was a lot of very casual sex for a number of years there. Looking back, I feel slightly embarrassed. On the other hand, do it while you can…

Unmarried mothers

Unmarried motherhood still carried a lingering stigma, although the winds of kinder change were stirring. But the norm was still to either have an abortion – if you had the nous and the wherewithal – or have the baby adopted.

Pregnancy was such a terrible, terrible thing to happen if you weren't married. It was talked about in whispers, and you reeled back in horror when you heard that so-and-so was pregnant. It happened to my cousin when she was sxteen, and it was the most awful thing for the whole family, a very significant event.

The girls who had babies while we were at school completely stuffed up their lives – their early lives, at any rate. You'd see them around town, dragging babies and pushing prams, looking about forty when they were nineteen. It was so sad.

I had a baby in 1966, when I was unmarried. That era, to me, was one of increasing tolerance. My parents were very tolerant, and I stayed at home the whole time. I did have pressure from social workers to have the baby adopted, but when I put my foot down they said 'Oh, OK', and it was fine. I didn't feel an outcast at all. This was the first time single mothers were tolerated, accepted. I never, ever encountered any attitude. It was starting to be the thing to do, then: film stars, and people in the limelight, were having kids without marrying the fathers, so it became more accepted. In the fifties, it would have been disastrous. So I'm very fond of the sixties.

None of us wanted to get pregnant. We wanted to be free. To live life. Then the magic drug came along just at the right time. But unmarried girls weren't allowed the Pill then. We just read about it in newspapers. Girls' magazines didn't write about contraception in those days. In March 1967, *Honey* ran their first feature on 'Birth control and the single girl'. I cut it out. Abortion didn't become legal until later that year.

People forget how conservative society at large was in the late sixties. In 1968, Dennis Tanner and Jenny Sutton of *Coronation Street* slept together before they got married, and there was such a stink in the papers.

I had an old Morris Minor, and several sexual episodes occurred in that. It was because you had nowhere else to go.

I had a gorgeous baby during my first year at university in 1965, she was absolutely lovely, but I didn't love her. I didn't find it at all traumatic to give her up for adoption. She'll be thirty-something now; she hasn't contacted me, and I haven't contacted her. I think I was too young and too selfish.

My friend Viv had a baby when she was seventeen, and we were all really amazed because we knew it had been conceived in a bubble car. I mean, how on earth do you manage to do it in a bubble car? But that was the only place they could go.

It was 1967, but before the Abortion Act, when I first became pregnant. I tramped around all the Harley Street doctors. I had to get a letter from a psychiatrist saying I was not fit to have a baby. That cost 10 guineas. Then the female doctor kept me sitting in the hall while she ate her dinner. She told me I was two and a half months, that she would book me in for the next week and that it would be 150 guineas – in cash.

I had an abortion in the late sixties, and I can remember sitting in a room in a Harley Street clinic where nobody else spoke English, but they were all clutching their cash. The girls were flooding across from Europe, because abortion hadn't been legalized anywhere else. You had to have two psychiatrists' reports, but they were all trumped up anyway.

As I left the abortion ward the doctor said, 'Take the Pill and don't come back.' I got back into the swing of life. There was no grief, nothing.

Wheels

For many of us, the sixties meant getting our own wheels for the first time. Scooters, motorbikes, cars... wheels meant mobility, wheels meant freedom. For James Bond wannabes, the E-type Jaguar was launched in 1960. But the ultimate wheels for ordinary young people – until Easy Rider made Harley Davidsons the Holy Grail in 1969 – was the Mini car, launched in 1962. Red was the preferred colour, of course. But we had little concept of socially acceptable driving...

Drunk driving just didn't seem to be a sin in the sixties. We all drank and drove. We drove while paralytic, at times. I remember once being a passenger in the back seat and thinking it a hilarious prank to put my hands over the eyes of the driver in the seat in front of me.

I borrowed my dad's Ford Anglia to go on holiday to Devon in 1967. On the motorway on the way there, we suddenly realized we were going the wrong way. So we just turned around, did a U-turn across the central reservation, and there was not a car coming in either direction, there was so little traffic in those days. In Devon we'd drink until we couldn't stand up, then we'd get in the car and try to drive back to the farm.

The days of old bangers went out with the MOT test, but in the sixties lots of people had cars that they'd bought for 50 quid. They weren't just mechanical wrecks, the bodywork had gone as well. Death traps. Doors had to be tied with string; floors had rusted through so you had to put metal plates over the hole or your feet would go through. Some grew fungus. And about 15 people would pile in. But there was hardly any traffic, so it was relatively safe to drive these cars around.

When mods grew out of scooters, they turned to motors. You had to have a Mini Cooper. You took the hub caps off and put wheel spacers on – which had the effect of making the whole thing structurally unsound, but that was neither here nor there. You had to have a straight-through exhaust pipe with no baffles, so it was really loud. And what you did on Saturday afternoons was, you belted up and down Guildford High Street, flat out in second gear, making as much noise as possible.

I had an Ariel Arrow motorbike, which was a 200 cc twin. Then I had a 500 cc Norton, with a state-of-the-art frame called a featherbed frame which was used on racing bikes. I even had one Japanese bike when they first came out, a Yamaha. It was a bit like riding a sewing machine – they made the same sort of noise.

Minis were really spunky little cars, but they were essentially city cars. They weren't meant to be driven all over Europe. We drove one to Rome in 1964 and had so many breakdowns on the way. We had to sell it in Paris on the way back to get the fare home.

I got my first car in 1968, a Morris Minor that cost me £30. I drove it in triumph down to London to show my parents, but had to be rescued by my father about 20 miles from home when steam started pouring and hissing out of the bonnet. We left it at a garage and went to pick it up the next day. I'd had no idea you had to check the radiator and top up the water, so of course it had run dry.

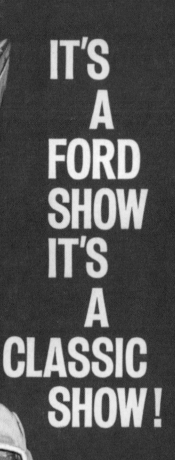

IT'S
A
FORD
SHOW
IT'S
A
CLASSIC
SHOW!

FORD
CAPRI
ZEPHYR
ANGLIA
CLASSIC

All the young men my friends and I knew had sports cars, mostly pretty cheap ones; it was the look that mattered, not the performance. Austin Healey Sprites were popular, and Triumph Heralds with no top. My friend Joanne had a Spitfire, and we'd drive around in that thinking we were the bee's knees, wearing sunglasses and headsquares.

The travel explosion

One of the innovations that differentiated the sixties from previous decades was the sudden availability of travel to the ordinary person. For the first time ever, families were able to holiday abroad; students of very little means headed off overseas; even travelling around Britain took on a new and exciting significance.

In 1964 I dragged my friend Marion off to hitchhike around France, so we could meet Sartre and become intellectuals. And we had nearly all our dreams fulfilled: we were arrested for sleeping rough under the bridges of Paris, and went around with this beatnik group. Oh God, it was everything I'd ever hoped for. It existed; it was out there. It was wonderful. Getting arrested was such a cachet, being herded into the police cell by these Parisian cops. And there were all these young people in France, sitting under the arches with their bell-bottomed jeans and long hair. It was like finding the Holy Grail.

Gaytours

sunshine holidays 1968

Gayflights from London Manchester & Newcastle

In 1965, two friends and I took a Mini all the way across Europe and down through Yugoslavia and into Greece. We spent seven shillings a day between us, and asked at the back of restaurants for their leftovers, that sort of thing; we were very proud of our Jack Kerouac approach to things, despite the Mini. Two of us had Beatle haircuts, and of course we had this Mini, which for many people overseas summed up that Swinging London thing. So there were parts of Greece, tiny villages and mountain towns, where the sight of the Mini would have the people pouring out into the streets. Then, when they saw that 'Beatles' were members of the crew of this little car, they went absolutely wild, and the most extraordinary generosity came our way. But at least three times a day we had to sing what we remembered of the Beatles repertoire.

I was a kitchen hand at Butlins at Barry Island in the three months between finishing school and going to university, in 1966. I had a brilliant time. There were lots of students from overseas there, and after my English upbringing, thinking we ruled the world, we were the best, it was a revelation. We'd been taught to hate the Germans, but I went to Germany after that stint at Butlins, to visit some people I'd met there, and I realized that they didn't hate us. They loved Bobby Charlton! It changed my life.

When we went to the South of France we used a tip given by Katie Boyle. She said, instead of using suntan cream, use olive oil mixed with vinegar. We were burnt to a crisp. Silly cow.

A group of us went on a camping trip to Turkey in the very first model Ford Cortina in 1964; an odd group, from Merseyside, South Wales, Lincolnshire. There were three of us from school, plus our music teacher and his girlfriend. We made a trip through places I'd barely heard of, like Romania, Bulgaria, Yugoslavia. It really opened my eyes to the fact that Britain was a tiny little place. We were astonished at the poverty.

In 1965 my boyfriend and I decided we'd go off and live in Greece for a while. We lived on Lindos, in a very arty community full of writers and photographers and poets and weavers. I felt a bit out of it, with my secretarial background, but I very much wanted to be in it.

During my first term at university in 1966 I went to Canada via BUNAC (British Universities North America Club) and promptly got pregnant via someone in Hamilton, Ontario, and had the baby adopted. There's a whole generation of adopted children out there.

We did a lot of hitchhiking. I remember hitching from Paris to Le Havre, and back from Southampton to Wales, regularly. It was quite normal then, but no one in their right mind would do it now, would they? Especially not girls or women.

The place to get adventure in 1967 and '68 was America, or at least abroad. Flower-power had hit America, but in English provincial towns such a romantic notion never really came to life.

I spent two summer seasons in Spain, in 1968–9. I drove down on my motorbike and worked in a bar in Fuengirola. I stayed nine months the second season, and it only rained for

one day the whole time. We rented a flat on Avenida de Mijas, starting with four of us, then, as we got greedy, it ended with about fifteen of us. But we weren't hippies: it was really difficult to be a hippie in Spain then. If anyone looked remotely scruffy they'd be kicked off the beach and hauled into gaol.

In the summer of '69 a group of us – five blokes and me – bought an old Commer van for £15 and set out for Spain. We only made it as far as Bordeaux before it conked out. Then I think we personally sank the AA's Five-Star insurance scheme, which we'd taken out before we left England for a couple of quid. The scheme paid for us to hire two cars to drive on down to Spain, where we stayed at a campsite for two weeks, living on bread and tomatoes and Cubalibres. Then it paid for all of us to get back to England by rail and ferry. The cherry on the pie was that it also paid to have the van towed back to England, where it arrived on our doorstep one day months later. It was a complete wreck, but there it was. We hadn't a clue what to do with it, so we ended up giving it to our landlord.

First jobs

I went to secretarial college in September 1960 for a year's course, which was very dreary. It covered not only shorthand and typing but also civics, office practice etc. They asked me what sort of work I'd like to do, and I said, well, I like reading. So they sent me to some publishing companies, and they all gave me interviews, and they all offered me jobs. Full employment, or virtually full employment, had a very big impact. I mean, to come out of some ordinary little secretarial college and just walk into a job in the area of your choice was what we took for granted. Magic!

I left school at sixteen in 1962. My mother arranged an interview for me with the local bank manager. I thought I'd work in the bank until I was eighteen, when I expected to go to teacher's training college. You only needed five O-levels to get in, then, and I had eight. But I ended up staying in the bank. I started work there at £350 a year, £6 a week, which was an amazing amount of money. I could do anything I wanted to on that amount, living at home. I never even considered leaving home, I didn't know about getting flats and things; it definitely wasn't an option.

I was always known as Miss Everett at work, and other people were called Mr So-and-So or Miss or Mrs So-and-So, even best friends. It's just the way it was.

In 1961 I earned 9 guineas a week, and I had a bedsitter in Hyde Park Gate that cost 3 guineas a week, which was precisely the recommended ratio.

In 1963 I decided I was going to live somewhere foreign, so I went over to Paris and got a job with the OECD at what seemed to me an extraordinary amount of money: I'd come from £9 a week, and they were offering me £20, tax-free, with a shop that sold tax-free grog and perfume, and a subsidized canteen where the food was fabulous.

LIBBY PURVES

Libby Purves, broadcaster and writer, was about to go up to Oxford in the late sixties. "I was a diplo-brat, and my parents were living in Hamburg, so in my gap year I worked for a German bank as a typist. This was a Bristow-like office where the men wore white nylon shirts and the women's skirts had to be over the knee and everyone was formally addressed—'Guten Morgen, Fraulein Purves'. Then I came over to London to visit my friend Fiona who was temping in Shepherd Market, Mayfair, and the culture shock was total. The ads in the tube said, 'Hey girls, like to work for two fun guys, Mikey and Dave?' It was like coming out of China. I watched Fiona's boss ask her to type something and she said, 'Piss off, baby.' And we'd walk down the King's Road in pelmet skirts and Courrèges boots and breathed the same air as Mary Quant. Everything in Britain seemed so laidback and unbuttoned, everyone just arsing around. So while Germany was creating an economic miracle, we slid majestically into our decline."

...DAYS I'LL REMEMBER...

When I left school at sixteen in 1964 I answered an ad in the *Evening Standard* for a receptionist/telephonist at an art publisher's in Kensington. They said, can you work a switchboard? and I said, yes (I'd never seen one before), and they employed me. The company was owned by chaps who'd been to Eton, the Guards, the City, then they decided that art would be a good thing to go into. It was all to do with that sixties thing of everything opening up. They'd always employed debs before, cousins of the Queen and so on. But they suddenly thought they'd get a prole, so they put an ad in the paper the very day I was looking. I was paid £6 a week. My weekly ticket to get from Raynes Park to Kensington cost something like 17/6, and I gave my mother 30 bob a week for my keep.

My first job after leaving school in 1965 was working as a stagehand at the Scala Theatre off Tottenham Court Road. The NATKE (National Association of Theatrical and Kine Employees, a powerful union now long gone) rate was 16/1d per performance; we got paid slightly under that, but there were phantom employees called Horatio Nelson and Napoleon Bonaparte, and you'd get someone to sign for them and you'd split their pay up between you.

My first paid full-time job, as opposed to Saturday work in shops, was as an unqualified temporary assistant teacher in 1966, between school and university. I worked in a girls' primary school in a fairly deprived part of London. The children were over 70 per cent immigrant, and many didn't know English. My first job was to take a group of them and try to teach them English. We had no classroom, so we sat on the stage in the school hall while P.E. lessons were going on around us. We mostly just sat and smiled at each other.

In 1966 I started a job in a merchant bank, which was the opposite of everything the sixties stood for. I was paid £1,000 a year as a clerk. I went to work every day in a white stiff collar with a stud, I had a very smart grey city overcoat and I was miserable. I had an adding machine at my desk, and I spent entire days counting either money or cheques or bills of lading. Just as the terrible constraints of workaday life in the city were clamping around me, I realized that this was the sixties, and if I wasn't careful it was going to be gone and I wouldn't have had much of it. The King's Road was there as a kind of terrific temptation; Carnaby Street was flourishing. So after 11 months of feeling miserable all week and freaking out at weekends, I resigned.

After I graduated in 1969 I did a secretarial course. That was the accepted route for a girl to take into a career, then: you did your degree, then you learnt how to type and take shorthand.

I wanted to go into journalism, and it was relatively easy to get into in those days. It was opening up for women, like everything else. At that stage, you still needed shorthand for journalism, so I did a course. I learned touch-typing too, and languages. It was great. I worked for the *Worcester Evening News*. The union rate set the same standards for men and women, so there was no discrimination in my pay. I also felt that I was on a par with my employers. There was no overt hierarchy, no forelock-tugging.

I spent the last three years of the sixties working for the *Spectator* in Gower Street, and I thought I'd gone to heaven. Work pretty well stopped at six, when the bottles of Teacher's came out in the editor's room. The editor then was Nigel Lawson, subsequently Chancellor of the Exchequer, and it was wonderfully friendly and convivial and nice, and literary. And although I was only paid £750 a year, it seemed like gold to me, because I was enjoying every second of it.

For my first job I wore very straitlaced, 'secretarial' clothes. I had long hair and wore it up in a backcombed, lacquered bun, because I thought that was what you did, until my boss said he couldn't stand women who put their hair up into buns. So I let it down, and never put it up again. We literally let our hair down in the sixties!

I wore a crimplene dress to my first teaching job in 1969. And I tied my long straight hair back with a shoelace. Such an old-fashioned, schoolmarmy thing to do. But I felt I had to conform to society when I started work.

Offices in the sixties were primitive compared with today. Hardly any had photocopying machines, so you had to use carbon paper between sheets of paper. If you made a mistake you had to rub them out and put a little piece of paper in between each sheet of carbon to type over it. And you did have to dress neatly. Women just didn't wear trousers in those days, not to work.

Sixties weddings – and beyond

The social climate was beginning to change. Girls no longer felt the same obligation to get married as soon as possible or risk being stigmatized as 'left on the shelf'. Nevertheless, shotgun marriages were still common, and the concept of women consolidating a career before getting married and having children was still fairly new. Many of us who did marry and start families in the sixties were conscious of missing out.

We had a good wedding. We'd all always said we'd never get married in a church, man, and all my friends did. But we were living in a crappy flat in Pimlico, and our local registry office was Caxton Hall. So we got married in

Caxton Hall. I was wearing an Empire-line purple corduroy dress from Fenwicks, which I edged with a gold braid. And I bought Chris a white suit, so he got married in white.

When we got married in 1969 we were both twenty-two, and I thought at the time how old we were. Now of course it seems so very young, doesn't it? I would be horrified if my own kids got married at that age.

We had two flats, one very little used. Mainly for parental purposes, but also for the landlord. We were paying £3/15s for one and £3/5s for the other. That was a lot of money in those days. That's partly why we got married in 1969: we were able to give up the £3/5s one.

I wasn't game to live with my boyfriend 'in sin', as it was known then, because I thought it would upset my parents. So we got married. It was very fraught, because we did it fairly quickly and my mother was in a total rage.

My son was born in 1968, and from then on the sixties sort of ended for me. That was it. I remember feeling a bit resentful that being a mother seemed to cramp my style a lot more than being a father did my husband's. And thinking, this isn't fair, I hadn't thought about this.

Women couldn't have babies then go straight back to work in those days. Even in London, there was hardly any organized childcare.

movements and shakers

make love not war

Politics

I remember hearing about Sharpeville, and Rhodesia. They were my first taste of world news. Television was so important in making us aware of what was going on. We might not have understood what was happening, exactly, but we got the gist and we were at least aware of the names. Whereas before, we hadn't had a clue.

JUNE 21, 1963 — ATLANTIC EDITION

CIVIL RIGHTS: THE MORAL CRISIS
"It is time to act in all of our daily lives."

TIME
THE WEEKLY NEWSMAGAZINE

BOBBY KENNEDY

Boycotting South Africa and not eating South African fruit was big in our house; my Uncle Tom got the film of the Sharpeville massacre out of South Africa. I went to a lot of demonstrations about that.

I remember the Cuban Missile Crisis of 1962 vividly, genuinely thinking that the world was going to end. Every night the news would come on with a map, showing how far the Russian ships had got towards the American blockade. You could predict the number of days it would take them to reach it. I remember thinking, I ought to do things now, because if the world is blown up I won't get the chance. The sense of relief was amazing, astonishing, when the Russians turned the ships back.

We were all very frightened about the Cuban Missile Crisis at the youth club one night. But it didn't stop us having our chips on the way home. I remember standing outside the chip shop discussing the end of the world. We thought Khrushchev was going to bomb the western world and that would be the end of it, wouldn't it? So you might as well have a bag of chips.

I remember being outraged when Harold Macmillan was suddenly ill and went, and everyone knew that Butler would be the next prime minister – and then somewhere, from some other world, they wheeled out the fourteenth Earl of Home, and he became prime minister. I was fifteen or so; there was Kennedy in the States who looked like a million dollars; and I thought, what a tired, pathetic, old country this is. I also thought this isn't right, this is not right, that the person who is in charge of our country a) is a lord, b) is a skeleton, and c) looks about 300.

I voted for Ted Heath the first chance I got. It was because I desperately wanted to be different, and everyone was very leftie at school. So I just went in the opposite direction. My idea of rebellion.

DAILY EXPRESS

No. 19,600   THURSDAY JUNE 6 1963   1 a.m. forecast: Sunny; thundery   Price 3d.

PROFUMO

He gives up War Minister's job and seat in House of Commons

QUITS: I LIED

His denial of impropriety with Christine Keeler was untrue... 'I misled you,' he tells Premier

PHOTONEWS As the bombshell explodes: Mr. Macmillan on holiday PAGES 4 & 5

Ricketts fails to convince Britain

Express Defence Reporter

Express Political Correspondent IAN AITKEN

MR. JOHN PROFUMO resigned from the Government last night, and will quit Parliament too—because, he admitted, he lied to the Prime Minister and the House of Commons when he said there was "no impropriety" in his relationship with model girl Christine Keeler.

The 48-year-old War Minister left his London home with his wife, former actress Valerie Hobson, a few hours before the announcement that shattered Westminster.

In a letter to Mr. Macmillan, Mr. Profumo said that by this deception I have been guilty of a grave misdemeanour.

He also mentioned rumours circulated three months ago about "the disappearance of a witness" and "some possible breach of security."

NO NAMES

Mr. Profumo gave no name, but was apparently referring to two people —

Christine Keeler, 21, who

Dear P.M.

MR. PROFUMO, from Chesterterrace, Regent's Park, wrote to Mr. Macmillan:—

Dear Prime Minister,

You will recollect that on March 22, following certain allegations made in Parliament, I made a personal statement.

At that time rumour had charged me

Mr. Profumo and wife, former actress Valerie Hobson

BACK-BENCH...

I can remember Nelson Mandela being imprisoned when I was in sixth form. It seemed so appalling.

The Profumo scandal of 1963 was the real change of the sixties. We lapped that up. It meant that what was good for the goose was good for the gander; it was the start of the crack in society.

England was just beginning to 'swing' – well, London was, at least – when the Profumo affair blew up and shocked our small town, because John Profumo was Stratford's MP. It was almost as if someone had written Peyton Place about Stratford and was pointing the accusing finger at all of us. We dug Stephen Ward – decadent, despairing, drugged! He fitted. But Christine Keeler had let our side down.

PRIVATE EYE

Price 1/-

Do you mind? If it wasn't for me – you couldn't have cared less about Rachman

Like everyone else, I thought Kennedy was the bee's knees. I wasn't really political, but I thought England was a tired country run by old people, and I thought America was an enterprising, ambitious country run by young people, and Kennedy symbolized that.

In 1964 our school, like hundreds around the country, had a mock general election, with a Labour candidate, a Tory candidate and a Liberal candidate. But we were unique in that we were the only boys' public school that returned a Labour candidate; we even made it into *The Times*.

The common rooms at university, which had been designed originally for drinking lots of beer and playing shove ha'penny, were suddenly covered in notices about Agitprop meetings, and you were expected to demonstrate against this or that politician or nuclear weapons, and so forth. There was quite a lot of action.

Churchill's funeral in 1965 had a huge impact on me. It felt as if it really was the end of an era. I remember people saying, 'Who's going to have the next State funeral? There isn't anyone worth having a State funeral for.' It was like Churchill was the last statesman Britain could produce, and that huge changes were about to happen.

I'd been very religious, then I turned to communism when I was about fourteen. I was a member of the Young Communist League, and went to Youth Parliaments and spoke for the communist cause – in Wimbledon! Bit of a lost one there. The local authority let us use the town hall for Youth Parliaments, it was a really big adventure. You'd go along once a month and sit in the council chamber, and there'd be the Tories,

TARIQ ALI

Tariq Ali was Britain's student revolutionary leader who led the anti-Vietnam demo in Grosvenor Square and edited The Red Mole *magazine.*

"The most amazing moment for me was when I received a little handwritten letter in the post at my college in Oxford, from the great Bertrand Russell – one of the philosophers we'd been studying – asking me to visit him. I went and had tea with him, and he asked me to go to Vietnam on behalf of his committee, and to set up an informal war crimes trial. It was the most incredible moment of my life. And having lived under American bombs for several weeks gave our anti-war demos a certain edge.

Later on, one of the best things was becoming friends with John Lennon after interviewing him for *The Red Mole*. He rang me and said he'd been so inspired by our talk he'd written a little song that we could sing on demos – and he sang it over the phone to me: it was 'Power to the People'. And Mick Jagger wrote me out a copy of his 'Street Fighting Man' too, with a note: 'This is the song the BBC are refusing to play on the radio.' So we published it in the magazine."

...DAYS I'LL REMEMBER...

the Labour Party, the Liberals, and the Communists. Goodness knows how we got in.

When the 1966 election results came in I was down at Trafalgar Square, watching the teleprinter, and people were jumping or being pushed into the fountains right left and centre. It was a bit like the end of World War Two.

One of the good things about university was the number of non-British people there. But I can remember the terrible fights during the Six Day War in 1967. These were people who had previously being doing the same course, and they were now almost having a surrogate war. Palestinian and Jewish students were at each other's throats.

I was involved in the Polaris marches, and the big anti-Vietnam War demonstration in Grosvenor Square. One of my friends was arrested for carrying a placard. A policeman broke it then said it was a dangerous weapon. I got hit over the head with a truncheon. It was very frightening.

In 1968 I went to the anti-Vietnam War demonstration in Grosvenor Square. And the big thing in the press was how the wonderful police horses were being brutalized by the bad guy demonstrators; but I can tell you that actually being charged by mounted police, by a cavalry charge... You'd been brought up to think of police as kind and civilized, helpful bobbies. Inside the demo you thought: these guys are prepared to kill me.

I went to America in 1968, and in Washington there were riot police with guns, shields, and a curfew after 10 o'clock. Another illusion of peace and love shattered. I was involved in a police intervention in a 'happening', and the organizer's wife kept calling the police 'pigs'. All the daffodils and other flowers in our hair would not have made for peace and love that night.

I went to America in 1968. I got a job as a *Sunday Times* researcher on the 'Insight' column for the Democratic Convention in Chicago. There was a counter-culture there, the hippie scene, but they were really serious. They were talking revolution, they were talking Weathermen and bombs. There was an odd mixture of what had been sheer hedonism in England, and a political element, SDS, Black Panthers; terrrifying, in a way. Chicago during the Convention, with the build-up of troops on Michigan Avenue, was the biggest crowd I'd ever been in in my life. I was down in the street opposite the Hilton, and there were people and tanks, and hippie girls putting flowers into gun barrels. I thought, something's going to go very badly wrong here. I had to go up to Newtown where they were tear-gassing students – absolute chaos. Terrifying.

SKETCH SOUVENIR FIRST MEN ON THE MOON

Daily Sketch

Monday, July 21, 1969   WEATHER: Dry, warm.   55   Price Fivepence

4 a.m. MAN TAKES HIS FIRST WALK ON THE MOON

Neil Armstrong steps from the Moonship in one of the last practice sessions before the mission.

From JOHN STEVENSON, Houston, Monday

MAN took his first steps on the Moon today. The time: 3.57 a.m.—nearly seven hours after Neil Armstrong and "Buzz" Aldrin touched down on the Sea of Tranquillity.

The two astronauts skipped their four-hour rest period to push ahead with the historic walk in the searing heat of the lunar dawn.

Armstrong emerged first, for a walk expected to last 2½ hours. As he left the Eagle spacecraft the temperature outside was around 150 degrees Fahrenheit.

Aldrin, remaining in Eagle for 25 minutes in case of an emergency return by his commander, started to run his 35mm movie camera.

HATCH OPEN

At 3.39 came the dramatic message the world was waiting for: Hatch is open.

"Put your left foot to the right a little" came Aldrin's voice as he directed Armstrong down the ladder.

"Takes a long time to get all the way down, doesn't it!" Armstrong remarked to Aldrin.

"Yeah," Aldrin replied.

First live TV pictures were flashed onto the world's screens at 3.55.

Armstrong's foot was seen poised above the rungs as he climbed down the ladder.

At 3.57 Armstrong stepped on to the moon's surface and said: "That's one small step for man."

Armstrong: "I can see the footprints of my tread in the fine powder.

"It's like a fine layer of powdered

I was in Paris in 1967–68, and it was wonderful realising that this huge mass movement of young people was happening there too. I missed out on the hippie drug thing – everyone was quite normal when I left England, and totally drugged-out when I got back – but I had the revolutionary thing instead. It was the last day to hand my dissertation in and I was running late. I got trapped in the courtyard of the Sorbonne then tear-gassed with student leader Daniel Cohn-Bendit.

They showed the moon landing on a huge colour TV in the foyer of my school, and I remember going to my aunt's place that night in Maidenhead, and while they were on the moon it was a big full moon over London.

RICHARD BRANSON

Richard Branson, global tycoon and balloonist, was a sixteen-year-old fifth-former at Stowe School in the summer of 1967 when he and fellow pupil Jonny Gems founded Student *magazine and ran it from the shambolic basement of the Gems' house in Connaught Square.*

"Getting Vanessa Redgrave to give us an interview was a turning point since we could use her name as a magnet to attract David Hockney, Jean-Paul Sartre, John Lennon, Mick Jagger... Peter Blake, who'd designed the 'Sergeant Pepper' album cover, drew a picture of a student wearing a red tie for our first edition. And by October 1968 all the staff of *Student* joined the march to Grosvenor Square to protest against the Vietnam war outside the American Embassy. I marched alongside Tariq Ali and Vanessa Redgrave. It was tremendously exhilarating to march for something I believed in, with tens of thousands of others. You felt at any moment that things could get out of control. And they did. When the police charged the crowd, I ran like hell. A photograph later appeared in *Paris Match*. It shows me, back arched, an inch away from the outstretched hand of a policeman who was trying to catch me as I sprinted across the square."

...DAYS I'LL REMEMBER...

SATURDAY,
NOVEMBER 23, 1963
THREEPENCE
No. 14840 •

Daily Herald

The life
and death
of a
President
Pages 2, 3, 4, 6

They rode in the car through the cheering crowds. The President and his wife. The Governor of Texas and his wife. Then bullets shot into the car. John Kennedy fell to the floor, dying.

Jackie cradles her husband after sniper blasts from window

ASSASSINATED!

Kennedy shot dead in car

From JOHN SAMPSON and ANTONY CURRAH
NEW YORK, Friday

PRESIDENT JOHN KENNEDY was assassinated today as he drove in an open car with his wife, Jackie, through the streets of Dallas, Texas. He was shot through the head by a hidden sniper and died in hospital about 30 minutes later.

Tonight, police in Dallas were holding a Communist, 24-year-old Lee Harvey Oswald on a charge of killing a policeman in a chase soon after the assassination. He is also suspected of killing Mr. Kennedy.

Oswald, a former Marine, defected to the Soviet Union in 1959, then returned to America last year. Two months ago he was arrested in New Orleans with several Cubans for circulating Communist leaflets.

Two policemen chased him into a Dallas cinema this afternoon. One of the officers was shot dead before Oswald was detained.

Mr. Kennedy, who was 46, was shot from a window on the fifth floor of an office building as he waved to cheering crowds. The bones from a meal of fried chicken were found in the building, indicating that the killer had been waiting there for some time.

HER RED ROSES

Police said tonight that Oswald was known to have been employed in the building. But he denied any connection with the assassination.

As President Kennedy fell, Governor John Connally, of Texas, riding in the same car, was also seriously wounded.

Mr. Kennedy crumpled face down to the floor of the car. His wife dropped a bouquet of red roses, went down on her knees and cradled his head in her arms, sobbing: "Oh no, oh no."

The car, driven by a Secret Service man, roared off to the nearest hospital, where Mr. Kennedy was given a blood transfusion.

Two Roman Catholic priests were called to his bedside, and administered the Church's Last Rites.

Mr. Kennedy—the fourth American President to be killed in office—is succeeded by Vice-President Lyndon Johnson, aged 55.

Mr. Johnson was sworn in as President at Dallas on the plane which flew Mr. Kennedy's body from the local airport to Washington.

As soon as the brief ceremony was over Mr. Johnson, obviously shaken, turned to officials and muttered: "O.K., let's get this plane back to Washington."

Mrs. Kennedy, silent with grief, was at the

Continued on Page Three

THIS IS SUSPECT No. 1

THIS is the man police suspect of shooting President Kennedy.
He is 24-year-old *Lee Harvey Oswald,* chairman of the U.S. Fair Play for Cuba organisation.
Oswald went to Russia in 1959 and said his departure from America was " like getting out of prison." He asked to become a Soviet citizen.
But the Russians refused permission and he returned to America last year with his Russian wife.
The couple have two children. Mrs. Oswald does not speak English.

' All over '

Police brought her to headquarters in Dallas last night and were preparing a list of questions to ask her.
Oswald has been charged with shooting a policeman who helped to arrest him in a Dallas cinema.
But police have not established whether he was the man who killed the President. Tests are being made for fingerprints on the rifle believed to have been used by the assassin.
Police quoted him as saying "It's all over now" as he was arrested.
Captain Will Fritz, head of the Dallas Homicide Bureau, told reporters: "He hasn't admitted anything yet, but he looks like a good suspect."

Lyndon Johnson takes the oath. By his side, Jackie Kennedy.

THE OATH AT A MOMENT OF GRIEF

A MAN, still half-numbed with shock, utters the words that establish him as President of the United States.
Lyndon Johnson takes the oath on board a plane at Love Field, Dallas.
By his side a grief-stricken Jackie Kennedy.
District Judge Sarah Hughes, weeping, holds the Bible with Johnson.
At the new President's right hand is his wife.

A vow

Soon President Johnson was on his way to Washington in the plane, which also carried the body of John Kennedy.
At Washington the new President spoke briefly of " a loss that cannot be weighed."
And he vowed: "I will do my best. That is all I can do. I ask your help—and God's."

THE MOMENT OF TERROR IN DALLAS..

Jackie Kennedy leaps up in the car as the President collapses. A security guard tries to help.

BERLIN MOURNS ON THE MARCH

EIGHTY THOUSAND people gathered around West Berlin's city hall late last night in a demonstration of grief at President Kennedy's death.
Thousands of them had marched with torches. A banner borne above them said: *President Kennedy is dead, but he will live in our hearts. He told us:* " *I am a Berliner.*"
President Kennedy won West Berlin's heart with those four words when he visited the city in June.
Mayor Willy Brandt, in a voice shaking with emotion, told the vast crowd last night: "I feel as if a light has gone out for all men who hoped for peace and a better life."
IN MOSCOW radio and television programmes were interrupted to give news of the assassination.

Man of peace

The Soviet Communist Party newspaper *Pravda* praised President Kennedy as a champion of peace. Mr. Krushev was reported to be hurrying back to Moscow from a visit to Southern Russia.
IN LONDON, the Football League sent out a message to all League clubs calling for a minute's silence before today's matches.
President Kennedy's sister-in-law, Princess Lee Radziwill, heard the news at her London home.
Today she flies to America to be with Jackie, her sister.
President Kennedy's sister, Patricia, wife of actor Peter Lawford, was last night under a doctor's care at her home in Santa Monica, California.
ON WALL STREET share values dropped by £3,000,000,000 on the news of President Kennedy's assassination.

'Where were you?'

The question 'Where were you when you heard that Kennedy had been shot?' (Friday 22 November 1963) has long been a catchcry of the baby boomer generation. It was such a seminal event, nearly all of us can remember where we were, what we were doing. Here's a selection.

Kennedy's assassination was a major event in my life. Mike Scott was on Granada TV's *Scene at 6.30* that Friday evening, and I was getting ready to go to the church youth club. At twenty to seven the phone rang on the news desk, and he picked the phone up and his face went absolutely white, and his mouth dropped open, and he didn't talk, he just listened. You couldn't help but watch, because he was obviously receiving some information that wasn't about the next bit of film being stuck or whatever. He put the phone down and said that information had come out of America that President Kennedy had been shot, and was possibly seriously hurt, but there was no real news about his condition. By twenty past seven, when I left, the news had been announced that he was dead. When I got to the youth club, everybody was crying. I don't think that would happen over a politician today.

My sister and I were getting ready to go to a dance at our school. I was putting on a particularly fetching orange outfit I'd made from an old dress plus some chiffon material I'd got in Spain that summer. Suddenly she burst into my bedroom with the terrible news, all tears and horror. I was a year younger, and far more concerned about the fact

that the assassination had ruined the evening. We went to the dance, but it was a very subdued affair. No fun at all.

I was at one of those dances in a village hall. There was a pathetic local rock group, playing sub-Merseysound. We sat around whispering; no one dared talk loud. But it was our Friday night out. We'd waited all week through school for this. Why should our Friday night dance be ruined because he'd been killed?

I was in my studio in Paris, and my Italian boyfriend rang me up to tell me the news. I was so shocked. We all had this fantasy about Kennedy and the new Camelot, didn't we? How they were both so young and glamorous and sophisticated, and into the arts, and different from their predecessors.

I was on my way to a Young Communist League meeting, and when I got there they were all glued to the telly, a tiny black and white set. Even though he was in many ways the enemy, Bay of Pigs and all that, it was beyond that, it was devastating.

Banning the Bomb

I really did think the Bomb would annihilate us all, that life held nothing for us. But I was too young to be allowed to go on the Aldermaston marches, so I marched at the front of the Newcastle chapter instead. It coloured all my thinking.

I remember the party in Burton where I first spotted a guy wearing not only a green parka but also a CND badge. It was the most exciting party I'd ever been to. There and then, in 1963, I promised myself I'd escape to London to be nearer those interesting men who belonged to CND and who lived dangerously. That badge symbolised a whole new intellectual world opening up to me.

My sister and I weren't allowed to go on the whole Aldermaston march, but we did join it for the final day one year. It was just wonderful. It would have been even more wonderful to have marched the whole way, and slept in a huge group in school

I was at Friday Night Club in Jackson's Lane, and someone came in and told us. We all thought something serious was going to happen; that the Russians had probably done it and they'd start fighting each other and that we'd all be called up.

I wasn't aware of anything much, I was just having a good time. I didn't care about Kennedy; it was America, a long way away, and it didn't affect me in the slightest.

halls and churches and things, but that one day was pretty good. Singing 'We Shall Overcome' and chanting and feeling very much a part of an exciting and morally correct movement.

I worried for years that it would be wrong to bring a child into a world that could be snuffed out in a moment. I genuinely thought people having babies were being selfish.

Worry about the bomb really did affect my life. There was a feeling of, it's all going to end soon in a nuclear holocaust, so what's the point of trying? It affected my school life, and my choice of career – or rather, my inability to choose a career. It all seemed so pointless.

The environment

In the bitter winter of 1962-3, I was coming up eighteen and the large lake at school froze over. We skated whenever we could, and it was an absolutely magical start to 1963. The whole of London was locked with massive snowfalls, and all the parks were chock-a-block with alpine mounds of ice, dug off the roads. We tobogganed on Hampstead Heath, and got chilblains.

I remember my uncle reading *Silent Spring* and talking about it in 1963, so I was aware of those concerns. There weren't any birds left in France, for instance, where my uncle lived, because they'd shot them all or they'd been poisoned by pesticides.

My sister and I met two American guys in Bulgaria in 1964, one of them a complete redneck. He had a four-wheel drive with a pair of antlers strapped to the front, and took us for a drive along the coast, during which he flattened every bit of greenery we came across. I remember thinking, hang on, this isn't right. It was my first lesson in ecology.

I arrived in Manchester in October 1965 and I didn't see it for a month. It was just a pea-soup fog. I had no idea where I was going.

We had to wear masks to walk to school during the smogs, in London.

We'd heard about that stuff they were dropping on Vietnam, and we wondered what that was going to do, but I don't think I was any more concerned about that than about Vietnam itself.

GYLES BRANDRETH

Gyles Brandreth, writer and broadcaster, was president of the Oxford Union in 1969 and later became a Tory MP.
"My problem with the sixties is that I remember it all with alarming clarity. As a decade it was completely wasted on me. I wasn't just a middle-aged teenager: I was positively elderly! My political heroes were Harold Macmillan, Sir Alec Douglas-Home and (God save the mark!) Edward Heath. Paul McCartney I met, but I still preferred the songs from 'Salad Days'. In 1968, when the students were manning the barricades, I went to Paris – not to join them, but to take tea with the Aga Kahn for the student magazine *Isis*.

In December 1969 I presented a TV show for ITV called *Child of the Sixties*. I sat on a stool and quizzed the great and the good of the day (Iain Macleod, Michael Foot, etc) about the great moments of the decade. I think the producers had hoped for a hip representative of the now generation. What they got was a know-it-all 21-year-old who thought he was Robin Day (without the bow-tie) with the mindset of Neville Chamberlain.

I do remember being offered a joint and declining it primly. I don't remember being offered free love – are you surprised? The point is: the sixties – I was there, but I wasn't, if you see what I mean. I've a feeling there may have been quite a few like me..."

...DAYS I'LL REMEMBER...

I think, for me, the sixties had nothing to do with anything that happened outdoors at all. Everything happened indoors. You were either in a flat or a house, a pub or a bar, a concert hall or a dance hall, or a lecture hall. Anything that happened outdoors – except sport – was anathema, it had nothing to do with our lifestyle at all.

Women's Lib

It took a long time to filter through to some of us. I mean, even though we'd been brought up to expect much more than our mothers had out of life, we still thought Benny Hill was funny, still thought it normal and acceptable for men to get better jobs than women. Until we hit the job market, and discovered that most of the male managers were far thicker than their secretaries (us, essentially).

When we were still at school we didn't want to be like the spinster schoolteachers, or what we still called 'blue stockings'. No girl dared mention the word career because 'career girl' was still the worst label to get thrown at you.

I went to a very strict, private girls' school, not at all academic, although I'm amazed at how much they taught us at the end of the day. But none of us was expected to take A-levels; it was assumed that we would leave school after O-level, dabble in something, then get married to rich men. You could be a nurse or a teacher for a while, but you weren't expected to have a career.

The summer before I left home to go to university, I remember looking out of my bedroom window into the office next door. I would stare at the girl sitting in there typing. She'd been at school with me, a bright girl who'd got her A-levels. Now she sat there at the typewriter with a big diamond ring glittering in the sunlight on her left hand. She was engaged. Her life now meant being in a secure job, eating sandwiches to save for the mortgage, and looking adoringly into her fiancé's eyes. I didn't want to know about any of that.

The worst thing about the mini skirt was it made you look like a little toy girl, just there to please men. Guys used to call us 'chicks' and 'birds', which I always hated.

I did wonder, in the mid-sixties, why the girls on the counter in the department store got eight pounds a week and the young guys got twelve pounds, for exactly the same work. It's funny looking back and thinking of working for unequal pay without a quibble.

As I became more political, I became aware that my mother was paid two-thirds of a man's wage in the factory, for doing the same job as the man sitting next to her.

One of the things that really bugged me in the sixties was that girls were expected to buy their rounds in the pubs the same as blokes, but we only ever had halves of bitter. I used to think, hang on, we should only have to buy half as many rounds, because all the blokes drank pints.

Quite a few pubs wouldn't let women in. Even when they did, they didn't allow women to drink out of pint glasses. There were ladies' glasses, like goblets, and if a woman wanted a pint the barman would pour out two halves into these goblets. My father would buy me two halves, but he wouldn't buy me a pint.

I remember being thrown out of – or, rather, turned away from – the Savoy for wearing trousers. This must have been about 1967–68.

My parents never encouraged me to have a career. It was seen as a complete indulgence for a woman to go to university because women's careers weren't considered important.

I was unsympathetic to the women's movement when it started, because I thought they just wanted a bigger slice of the capitalist pie, when in my opinion the whole pie recipe ought to be changed. My view was a hangover from the simple hippie lifestyle thing.

The class system

I suppose I was quite bitter when I was young. I had a bit of a chip on my shoulder. I was from a very working class family – I was the first person in my family to stay on at school after the age of fifteen. I might have been a bit bolshie, a bit difficult. I still feel that way now, I still spend half my time at work feeling angry, feeling 'I can take you'.

I developed my idea about class enemies very early; I hated loads of people. I read things like Trotsky when I was about fourteen – people did, then. I can't imagine fourteen-year-olds reading stuff like that now. It made me angry.

In the early sixties, the class system remained absolutely intact. We moved to Essex in 1964, thirty miles outside of London, and my mother's daily cleaning lady – who always called me 'Young Sir' – had never been to London. Her husband always tugged his forelock.

When it got to about 1965, you began to get this extraordinary new mix of older, quainter aristocracy, who became suddenly pop, and pop became the new upper class. You had characters like Tara Browne, one of the heirs to the Guinness fortune, who was killed in Whitehall when he crashed his car; he was great friends with the Rolling Stones. The mix of the old world, where people lived in big country houses and the squire had a butler, and the new order of pop stars, still held even at the end of the sixties. Having a title was still terribly important, and pop stars bought big country houses and aspired to be lords of the manor.

There's no way Noël Coward was an ordinary guy, but suddenly here's Cilla Black, the Stones, Cathy McGowan, all fundamentally ordinary people just like you and me, becoming celebrities. We all felt just one step away from stardom, which was a hideous lie.

In the sixties we were all liberal and left-wing and we didn't believe in class and we all favoured the idea of comprehensive schools. But the fact is that the scene at the Oxford college balls was one of the old middle-class meritocracy in their evening dresses and dinner jackets down on the dance floor, looking pretty posh, and up on stage were the representatives of the new rebellious working class, who dressed down, looked crazy, drank on stage and were no doubt doing other things as well. They represented freedom and subversiveness to us.

Because of the relative narrowness of communications, what you had is an enormous cultural cohesion. The Beatles and the Stones were recognized and loved nationally. Everybody under a certain age liked them.

There wasn't this fantastic difference between people who liked hip-hop and garden and hothouse and garage and the this, that and the other that you have now. Everybody under twenty-five had to watch *Ready, Steady, Go* on Friday night, and there was a shared injection of excitement, which went all around the country. The young were pulling together, possibly for the first time in history.

We were all pulling away from the Establishment. I was brought up in this very poor working class home, but my mother voted Tory. The stock she came from was very much the deserving poor: they kept their children clean and did well for themselves, all had little businesses and went up the scale a bit. I remember her eyes glazing over as I tried to instruct her in the ways of socialism.

I think there was a lip service to being democratic. It was playing at it. It was a big shock to realize that the class system wasn't breaking down after all. I'm astonished now how little alliances have shifted over the years. But it felt as though it was going when the Labour Party got in, and everybody, all the Hons and such, were thrilled. Except they weren't, really.

ED STRAW

Ed Straw is the chairman of Relate (the Marriage Guidance Council).
"The sixties were our world, our time, an end to more mind-numbing mores than I care to recall. The contrasts were stark. Leaving a traditional public school (an emotion-free zone) and growing long hair and a moustache. Jimi Hendrix struck the first chords of 'Hey Joe' on *Top of the Pops* and my soul said hello. Freedom, power, invention, genius. Was it only jealousy which provoked the later knocking of such heights?"

...DAYS I'LL REMEMBER...

Sport

The 1966 World Cup was magic. But watching the final I assumed, sadly, that it was another world war. When the Germans equalized I thought that was absolutely bloody typical of them. I remember the Russian linesman, and the tension waiting for that decision. But the thing I most remember, along with everyone else, is Kenneth Wolstenhome saying, 'The people on the pitch think it's all over. It is now.' I thought at the time, what a brilliant thing to say. Ever since then, commentators have been trying to say something equally memorable so they will go down in posterity.

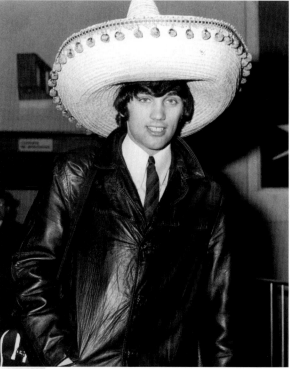

I went to the quarter-final between Uruguay and somebody. After about ten minutes Uruguay had eight men; three had had a fight and been sent off. I had a complete sense of betrayal, because you'd gone to this big match and it was ruined.

There weren't many people on the streets when England was playing games in the World Cup. It was a great time, wasn't it? Until the next World Cup, when we just went back to normal.

Being in Manchester when Best, Law and Charlton were playing for United was amazing. You were looking every week at the three best players in Europe. George Best was the first player to take football further than sport and become a fashion trendsetter, sponsoring products and making millions. He was a first, just like the Beatles and Dylan. A product of the times.

I think Gary Sobers is one of the best human beings ever to have lived. And to have seen Gary Sobers play…I found county cricket in those days a bit too slow. At Lord's, there'd be about three people in a ground that could hold 50,000. Rain always stopped play, and there'd be no result. It was deadly dull. So the one-day games made cricket much more attractive to people like me.

I remember when Cassius Clay fought Henry Cooper at Wembley Stadium and Cooper came very close to winning. He belted Clay with a left hook and put him on his pants. But the bell went and there was a huge delay while a mysterious split glove was replaced, and Clay had time to recover. Cooper used to get cut very easily, and Clay managed to open a huge cut over one of Cooper's eyes and that was it. Cooper got a shot at the title a couple of years later, this time at Arsenal Stadium, but again got cut around the eyes. Elizabeth Taylor and Lee Marvin were at the ringside and they got splattered with blood.

Moving on

Although the sixties didn't really turn into the seventies until about 1973, by the end of 1969 we knew times were changing again. After Woodstock came Altamont – for many, a symbol of the death throes of the Swinging Sixties.

Although I was unaware of the passing of an era, I was very much aware of the end of the sixties because halfway through 1969 I finished college and had to face the real world for the first time. It was like the end of the best party ever held. I started a job on 1 January 1970, and nothing was ever as carefree and intoxicating again. The whole world suddenly felt like the morning after.

Universal Electronic Vacuum – hip or what? – which cost about £500 for a set of ten. And I remember someone coming and buying a set, and I said how do you want them framed, and they said, oh no, they were going straight into storage as an investment. That was the moment I realized the whole thing was turning.

In summer 1967 I worked a harvest, and one of the farms had an old guy who still made sheaves. Where we lived in London, there was still a lamp-lighter who rode a bicycle around, lighting the gas lamps. Steam trains died out in the sixties; the Evening Star was the last steam locomotive built in England. All the branch lines disappeared. A whole lot of things vanished, a whole society, a whole culture.

We had the most wonderful parties and happenings at the art gallery where I worked. That was the way it was, wasn't it? Lots to drink, lots of food, lots of money sloshing around; 'let's have a good time'. It was just extraordinary, the amount of fun it was. But I remember when it all died for me, at the end of the sixties. We'd published a big set of wonderful prints called

For me, the end of the sixties was the end of student life, and the beginning of a married life and a career as a teacher. A very significant change.

recipes with Nimble bread.

So many diets are based on substitutes for proper food. Nimble is delicious, real fresh bread, but bread baked lighter so it's designed to fit neatly into a calorie-controlled diet—and so to help you slim.

But because Nimble tastes so good, it's bread that the whole family will enjoy—especially toasted for breakfast—yet one slice of Nimble contains only 40 calories, compared to 67 for ordinary bread.

Nimble

NEW

Nimble

only 40 calories a slice

is a lovely way to slim

All good things come to an end, don't they?